A BOOK FOR ALL FAMILIES

Twelve Life Lessons from a Coach, a
Teacher, and a Parent

YOUR VERY OWN *PERSONAL BEHAVIOR MAP*
TO SELF-FULFILLMENT

By

Harvey D. Heartley

Foreword by
Coach Dean Smith

To Walt
Keep on helping
our Youth

Coach Heartley

8-23-03

A BOOK FOR ALL FAMILIES

Twelve Life Lessons from a Coach, a Teacher, and a Parent

YOUR VERY OWN PERSONAL BEHAVIOR MAP TO SELF-FULFILLMENT

EMPHASIS ON THE "SPEMPP – FAR – SIS"

By
Harvey D. Heartley

ISBN: 0-9717383-0-0

Additional copies of this book are available by mail. Send $14.95 plus $4.95 for shipping and processing to
HDH PARTNERS, INC.
311 New Bern Avenue
Post Office Box 26381, Raleigh, NC 27611

Printed in the United States by
Morris Publishing
3212 East Highway 30
Kearney, NE 68847
1-800-650-7888

DEDICATION

This book is dedicated to my wife, Maria, and my four lovely children (Delphyne; Harvey, Jr; Shawn, and Gregory); the late great basketball coach and my mentor, Dr. John B. McLendon; all of my family members (especially my mother, father, and brothers) past, present, and future; and all of my fellow coaches, players, co-workers, students, and friends who have taught me most of the lessons found in this book. It is also dedicated to the Saint Augustine's College family, which gave me the opportunity to grow and help contribute to the college, the community, and the nation. I have the deepest love and appreciation for you all, and I truly love you all!

FOREWORD

A BOOK FOR ALL FAMILIES is a great
testimony to Coach Harvey Heartley, a man I
have known for over 30 years as a man of
honest character and integrity. His twelve
life lessons give enlightening and
practical perspectives on fundamental
issues we all face in the course of living.
It is well worth reading.

In these challenging days of family
uncertainties, Coach Heartley gives
detailed explanations and suggestions as to
how to master problems that have existed
over time. These same issues will persist
in the future, regardless of race, culture
or ethnic backgrounds.

I highly recommend this book for every
individual to read and share with his or
her families, friends and co-workers. It
is an excellent book with a unique, sound
approach to winning in life. Coach
Heartley's suggestions are sensible and
applicable to all people in any aspect of
life.

Congratulations, Coach, on this
distinguished achievement.

Dean Smith
Basketball Coach Emeritus
The University of North Carolina

PROLOGUE

Harvey Heartley has written a most inspiring personal treatise, filled with humor and wit. His book, **A Book For All Families**, is the result of a lifetime of personal study and application of genuine wisdom. In this creative work he engages in the process of personal development of himself and the reader. This interactive style is the result of his experiences as a world traveler, social leader, political mediator, civic organizer, financial advisor, motivational lecturer, recreational icon, and astute mentor. Harvey's conversational tone makes the reading enjoyable and has a wide audience appeal.

This book has been an ongoing process over a number of years, as I have personally been blessed to witness during the twenty years I have known and been married to him. His adoring children also have benefited from his guidance and wisdom. The work is genuinely "Harvey Heartley," for he speaks from the heart. Harvey lets the reader in on his secrets for living a wholesome and productive life. Families, without regard to race, creed, class or nationality, will enjoy this book, which shares generational wisdom. His philosophy of life is that "attitude determines altitude." Therefore, it is necessary to maintain a positive outlook on life, which radiates from within to the world without. He uses artistic license to call this comprehensive philosophy SPEMPPFARSIS, which is an acronym for Spirituality, Physical fitness, Education, Mentality, Politics, Professionalism, Financial matters, Attitude, Relationships, Sociality, Imagination, and Sensuality, the names of chapters in the book.

All of the aforementioned attributes have been deeply etched upon his character and have given him a healthful perspective on life. The outflow is what he calls his infinite processing and is what gives the book its particular and universal appeal. It is a great contribution to the personal essay genre.

Loving wife,
Maria L. Heartley

TABLE OF CONTENTS

THE *REAL* DAILY DOZEN

"S P E M P P-F A R-S I S"

LIFE'S TWELVE DEVELOPMENTAL TASKS

INTRODUCTION

Do what you can with what you have where you are now!

I have always written things down. When I coached basketball teams, I kept a log of each game as it went along. People would say to me, "What are you doing sitting over there writing during the game?" I wrote down every aspect of each game: the names of the members of the opposing team and the names of our players; our defensive and offensive plans; the heights and weights of each team's players, and their relative strengths and weaknesses; the officials (in case I needed to second guess them), etc. And then I documented every play of each game. At timeouts and at the half, I would relate to our players exactly what had happened in the game so far and, based on those observations, I would diagram the plays and tell them what our strategy would be for the second half. At the end of each game, whether we won or lost, I would write it all up while it was fresh in my

1

mind so I would have something to study before the next time we played them. I literally kept a diary of all my coaching experiences, and learned from each one of them.

I did the same thing in the other areas of my life. Each month I have tried to look back over the previous month and understand what was good and what was not. Now I do it each night and each morning when I get up. At this stage of my life, I don't write down as much, but every morning when I wake up I think about what I did yesterday that was good or bad, and what I am going to do today. I keep a daily schedule of what I need to get done.

Even with all this planning and reflection, life is often a paradox. No matter how well I plan, there are always things that will throw my plan out of kilter. I know that there is no perfect way to live my life, but I have found ways to enable myself to function at my best, and I have shared my experiences and life lessons with countless others over the years. Family, friends, students, co-workers, and several fellow coaches have encouraged me to "put all of this together in a book."

Former students have come back to see me years after they graduated and said, "Remember that day you told us . . . ." and they will relate some lesson I passed on to them. "It struck a cord for me then, and you really got me started." Most of the time I will have completely forgotten the incident.

Two experiences that occurred many years apart made me decide to write this book and formalize these life lessons. First, when my mother died in 1986 and we held the celebration of her life, I realized the extent to which she had affected the lives of so many people. When my father died ten years later, we found a big file cabinet with a history of the family and also the history of our church. It had information about my great-grandparents and many other relatives; and because this history was written down, we were able to pass it on from one generation to the next.

In October 16, 2000, my wife and I attended the Million Family March in Washington, DC, and as I looked around at the thousands of people of all ages, backgrounds and religions, it occurred to me that we all shared something in common: we were all searching for some answers to the problems in our family lives today. That weekend, as I walked around and listened and spoke to people there, I realized that the great gifts I had been given - wise and caring parents, grandparents and a loving wife who helped me develop my own life philosophies and beliefs - should be shared with the many others who may not have had the benefits I have had. So this is a legacy that I want to share with my family, friends, all my many students, my athletes and those readers whom I have never met personally but who could use some insight and guidance in this difficult but wonderful thing called living.

This is not a typical self-help book. There are no set formulas for how to change your life. In fact, I encourage all readers to challenge and disagree and, ultimately, come up with their own views and philosophies about the topics covered.

It is not a "health" book although at its most basic level it is a book about how to cope with and minimize the stress in your life.

4

It is not a "philosophy" book, but I do share with readers my philosophies in many different areas and I ask that readers think about and write down their own philosophies while reading the book, and write them in this book.

It is not a "religion" book although there are numerous references to a Supreme Power or Being. My own background and upbringing is Baptist, so my life experiences and observations come from that realm, but each reader must experience this book through the lens of his or her own spiritual senses. Those readers who do not relate to the spiritual aspects of living can simply adapt the lessons here to their own experience and beliefs. There is no right or wrong way to experience this book.

This book is a conversational essay. I do not ask readers to accept what I say here, just to listen and evaluate. Every reader will take away a different set of lessons from this material. I wish I could simply sit down and talk to each reader individually, as I have done with my family, my children, my students, friends and colleagues. The next best

5

thing is writing it down for all to read on your own. I would like for this to be a reference book – something you refer to again and again over the years.

Life is not a destination but an endless journey. Enjoy the ride to Infinite Processing.

HOW I LEARNED ALL THIS

This book reflects my philosophy of life – my views on how to live a fulfilling, happy and meaningful life. Many people don't think they have a philosophy – of life or anything else. I didn't give it any thought when I was a young man until I had an experience that made me stop and reevaluate things.

When I first started coaching basketball, I had a job in a small rural town. I thought I was coaching, but I was really just having fun. I coached both men and women, and I found myself playing along with the team. I was spending a lot of time with them, but when we got ready to play, I found out that my players were not prepared to compete. That was a "wake-up call" for me. I realized I had to organize practices and myself because there were basic things that the players needed to know. I got a book on the administration and supervision of physical education and athletics, and it said that before you start anything you have to have a philosophy of sport. So I sat down with some more books and read about the philosophies of most of the great basketball coaches, and I wrote out my own philosophy.

I had learned self-discipline from my mother, who trained me to help her in many areas of our lives while my father was away in World War II. That same discipline helped me to organize my thoughts and prepare my team to play real basketball in a competitive way. From that lesson, I began to look at other areas of my life and realize that I needed a philosophy for each major element. Over the years I've learned many lessons and I've refined my philosophies about many things, but I have never stopped believing in the importance of having a philosophy on different things and living by it. That's the ultimate lesson of this book. Whatever your philosophy may be, recognize it and live by it. If you don't have one, now is the time to take aim, think and form one.

BASIC GUIDELINES FOR LIFE

There are certain points that I make throughout this book, and I thought it would be helpful to summarize them up front. They are basic guidelines for life. Take a look at them here because you will see them again and again in this book.

Infinite Processing

We are all students of life for life. Learning and growing never end. Life is a process, and you can process to any level that you are willing to work to. There are no limits except the limits that we put on ourselves. I call this **Infinite Processing**, and it's an important concept to keep in mind. Remembering that you're always learning will make you handle situations differently. It will make you think about what lesson life is teaching you at this moment. It will keep you constantly inquisitive and open to new thoughts and ideas. It will also make you a more interesting person to others. And most important of all, it will enable you to enjoy life to its fullest because learning and growing is more fun than stagnating.

ICE (Intergenerational Collaborative "Entergy")

This book is for all age groups - all generations. Throughout it you will see references to how one generation can help another one and the importance of having all generations working together. I believe that the most effective way to help young people develop into the productive, contributing adults we want them to be is to enlist the help of their elders. Young people watch their elders and they act - or react - based on what they see. By having the parents, family members and grandparents of young people involved in their development - sharing their goals and participating with them in growth activities - we can accomplish a lot. Not only will young people feel the support of their families and their communities, but also adults will feel more involved in the lives of their children and will grow and learn along with them. When everyone is having fun together, great things can happen. You will see throughout this book how I look across generations to solve problems. This is the ICE concept. *ICE - Intergenerational Collaborative EnTergy (the "T" stands for "team") - it works.* It denotes TEAM ENERGY: everybody working together to accomplish team-oriented goals.

The Paradox of Life

Life is a paradox. Regardless of how well we plan, there will always be things that throw our plans out of kilter. Throughout our lives, we encounter instances when things just don't make sense. We naturally look for the logical, "right" answer to life's questions, but there often just isn't one. The reason is that all of life itself is a paradox. Something can be both right and wrong depending on the view and/or the situation. Things can be different than they seem. The importance of this lesson is that we need to learn to be comfortable with that. Life is surprising and paradoxical. Get used to it. It keeps things interesting.

11

It's not always either/or; it can be
either/or/and.

30-Day Plan

Habits can be learned and broken
in approximately 21 days. If there's
something in your life you'd like to
change, give it 30 days. Make the
changes and stick with them for a
month. You'd be amazed at how much
change can happen in that short
period of time. I learned this many
years ago, and I taught hundreds of
students how to make a 30-day plan.
It's something you'll read about over
and over in the chapters of this
book. Try it.

Get Rid of the "Thought Police"

All through our lives, starting
with when we are children, we are all
sort of brainwashed about what we can
and can't think, what we can and
can't believe. It's a subtle thing;
we're often not even aware of those
monitors in our heads telling us what

thoughts are off limits – which ones are not allowed.

I was fortunate as a child to have parents and grandparents who encouraged me to challenge and question things. Even when I went way beyond what they believed, they didn't tell me what to think and what not to think. That was a valuable lesson that I want to pass on to readers of this book. When you let the thought police censor what you think, you cheat yourself out of drawing your own conclusions – thinking for yourself.

Whenever you sense that your thoughts are being influenced by the thought police, get rid of it, and let your thoughts run free. Only you know what's right for you based on your own philosophies of life.

HOW TO USE THIS BOOK

This is a book that helps you look at where you are – how your life is going – and make some changes if you need to do that. It's not a "Bible" or anything etched in stone, but it gives you an idea of how to explore the various aspects of your life. And it lets you know where you can go – in the family, in the community, in the church, in school, and on the job. There are always people out there who can help you move up to the next level. *My philosophy of life is Infinite Processing. You never get there, but the pleasure is in the journey. This is an eternal journey. You never cease to exist.*

Sometimes we get out of balance, and our psyche has a way of letting us know that something is not right. Often we don't know what the problem is. Sometimes it's obvious: if you don't feel good, it's probably physical. If you're having trouble with money, you know it's financial. But there are problems on some levels that are not as obvious; all you know is that something is just not quite right. So what do you do? That's where this book can help. Its purpose is to make you aware.

First, you want to try to identify the area of the problem: is it a problem with relationships? Is it one of spirituality? Once you've identified it, you need to make sure you are defining it correctly. The empirical meaning, or how it's described, is in the dictionary. Describing it is the first thing to learn. Then you have to figure out what you interpret from it. Also, try to figure out what others interpret from it. Then you'll know you're talking about the same thing, or you can tweak the meaning such that you can agree. Next, explore how you feel about it: what are your values about these things? How do you relate to them? *How do they affect you in your day-to-day living? That is your philosophy*. Once you understand your own philosophy, then you can better understand the situation and how to deal with it.

This book helps you through that process. For each of the *"Real Daily Dozen,"* I have included the definition according to Webster, and I've also talked about my own philosophy. Many people don't even know that they have a philosophy. The fact is, they just don't know that it exists; a philosophy always exists. Once we realize that everybody doesn't have the same definition and philosophy that helps explain some of the problems we have with other people. When you talk to people you have to first see how they define the issues and whether you define them that same way. Then if you're going to have interactions or relationships, you have to come to some type of agreement as to how you both are going to define them, although they might not be defined the same way in different areas.

Although I don't think there is a specific hierarchy to the various aspects of our lives, I do think spirituality, physicality and financial issues are probably more important than the others. If your spiritual life is in order, you're physically fit and financially sound, then you can more easily deal with the other aspects of your life. These three are the linchpins of the whole thing. Although they are all important, if you can take control of these three, then you can fine-tune the others.

Of course, if one aspect of your life is way out of kilter, it can affect the rest of your life. What I'm trying to do here is not only get you to look at yourself, but to look at your family, your job, your community, your country, and the whole world from the same definitions and the same philosophies. This is because if we're defining something differently – if I think I'm defining spirituality one way and you're defining it another way – then we're not really talking about the same animal. If I believe one thing, you believe something else, and the people in Greensboro believe something different from what we believe, I still need to know what they're thinking. This is because, if I interact with them, in order for me to understand where they're coming from and use the same language they use, I've got to understand their views and be able to resolve differences between us. I can do that either by changing my views or convincing them to change theirs or maybe coming up with some kind of compromise in which we take the best of both views.

I'm not for creating problems for people, but I won't have certain things forced on me. Then again, how you react to people and things depends upon your independence, and in a capitalistic society, independence usually means how much money you have and whether you are able to live without the support of those other people. If you're not, then you have to be pragmatic at times, because certain financial restraints will keep people from doing certain things. I'm not trying to put anyone into a situation where they have to damage relationships or put their job or financial situation at risk just because they have a certain philosophy about something. You have to be able to look at a situation and know when you should do or say certain things. Ultimately, if you're going to be healthy, you will have to resolve those situations as best you can.

None of this is to be forced. None of this do you have to do. Readers will probably find that out of my "real daily dozen," they might have some other aspects they break out differently than the way I break them out. If you feel good with that, well then break it out your way. You don't have to limit them to twelve and you can combine some of them. *It's just that these areas exist.* Recognizing this makes life more meaningful. It gives you a chance to keep on top of things that make your life pleasant and to deal with things that don't.

So I encourage readers to use this book as a way to look back over their lives to see where they are, to see where they want to go, and what philosophies they have. Are you defining things the right way? Is this really what you thought it meant? This book is just a guide to help you through that process.

Some readers may want to read the book straight through while some others might choose to skip around depending on the particular area they need help with. Any way you choose to use the book is fine. And after you've finished reading it the first time, consider it a reference book and pull it out when new problems arise, or when you think you need some extra help evaluating where you are. After all, the process of learning and growing never ends. Each of the Real Daily Dozen has been researched and widely discussed in library books. Check them out, read them, and use them as resource lessons. This book is not a dissertation on these parameters but a guide to point you to the places you can go to get deeper meanings.

A

QUICK-LOOK

MANAGEMENT GUIDE

TO

GAIN CONTROL OF YOUR

TIME
HEALTH
EDUCATION &
FINANCES

POST ON YOUR REFIGERATOR DOOR

Time is one measure of life. Time wasted is life wasted. Time saved is life saved. Effective use of time, like effective use of money, is one way to find more enjoyment and more success from our daily living. Each of us has at his or her command the same amount of time for each week--exactly 168 hours; no more, no less. Thus it is not the amount of time, but WHAT YOU DO WITH YOUR TIME that counts most.

The secret of more effective use of time and greater enjoyment of living lies in organizing and planning. Each person will, of course, plan his or her own 168 hours to harmonize with his or her unique requirements, inclinations and interests. But there can be no doubt that wise planning for the use of your time will provide more time for those things you are interested in doing. Each thirty minutes saved through planning is time that can be used to make life richer and better.

Time planning is no magic formula. Its value depends upon study, thought and effort. The plan suggested here could be a valuable asset to anyone who has the self-discipline to carry it through. To make it work for you, however, you cannot give up and quit after a half-hearted initial effort.

DAILY/WEEKLY ACTIVITY SCHEDULE

Week

of_____

Time	Monday	Tuesday	Wednesday	Thursday	Friday	Saturday	Sunday	Time
6:00 6:30	GET	UP	EVERY	DAY	AT	SAME	TIME	6:00 6:30
7:00 7:30								7:00 7:30
8:00 8:30								8:00 8:30
9:00 9:30								9:00 9:30
10:00 10:30								10:00 10:30
11:00 11:30								11:00 11:30
12:00 12:30								12:00 12:30
1:00 1:30								1:00 1:30
2:00 2:30								2:00 2:30
3:00 3:30								3:00 3:30
4:00 4:30								4:00 4:30
5:00 5:30	WORK	DAY	USUALLY	ENDS		BETWEEN	5 & 6 PM	5:00 5:30
6:00 6:30								6:00 6:30
7:00 7:30								7:00 7:30
8:00 8:30								8:00 8:30
9:00 9:30								9:00 9:30
10:00 10:30	GO	TO	BED		BETWEEN	10 & 11	PM	10:00 10:30

d

SOME WELLNESS TIPS

1. Avoid cigarette smoking and all tobacco products.

2. Avoid drinking alcoholic beverages or drink no more than one or two drinks a day.

3. Eat a variety of foods each day, especially quantities of fruits, vegetables, whole grain breads, cereals and lean meats.

4. Limit the amount of fats, salts, spices and sugars.

5. Drink at least eight glasses of water.

6. Maintain a desired weight; be neither underweight nor overweight.

7. Follow your designed fitness program (30-60 minutes daily or at least four times per week).

8. Have a worthy use of your leisure time. Participate in family and community activities often.

9. Limit prescription drugs intake to that prescribed by your doctor.

10. Do not do illicit drugs of any kind.

11. Always wear your seat belt and make sure others in the car do also.

12. Get eight hours of sleep daily.

e

A DO IT YOURSELF FITNESS PROGRAM

	<u>First Month</u>	<u>Second Month</u>	<u>Third Month</u>
Warm –up	15 min. jog	15 min jog	15 min. jog
Stretching	10 min. upper body 10 min. lower body	10 min. upper body 10 min. lower body	10 min. upper body 10 min. lower body
Work-out	5 push-ups	15 push-ups	30 push-ups
	25 crunches	35 crunches	50 crunches
	20 arm curls	30 arm curls	45 arm curls
	5 pull-ups	15 pull-ups	30 pull-ups
	20 leg curls	40 leg curls	50 leg curls
	10 squats	40 leg extensions	50 leg extensions
	1-mile run	20 squats	35 squats
Cool-down	15 min. jog	15 min. jog	15 min. jog
	5 min. walk	5 min. walk	5 min. walk
Stretching	10 min. upper body	10 min. upper body	10 min. upper body
	10 min. lower body	10 min. lower body	10 min. lower body

f

	Amount/owe	Paid	Balance Due	Comments and Check #s
I. INCOMES				
II. NECESSITIES				
Food	CASH			#2394
Rent	632.00			#2399
CP & L	141.00			#2396
PSNC	26.66			#2411
City H2O & Sewage	(7-25-00)	41.02		#2395
House Phone	23.19			#2402
Company Phone	22.67			#2409
Cell Phone	32.54			
Auto. Insurance	986.35			
Auto. Maintenance		293.84		
Home Maint./Repair		186.37		
III. SAVINGS 10%				
IV. INSTALLMENTS		10%		
American Express				
MasterCard				
Citibank				
V. FUTURE PROJECTS				
VI. OTHER ITEMS				
Man's Health Mag.	24.97			#2398
Falcon's Foundation	100.00			#2400
Rodale Book "(AGE PROTECTORS)"		29.45		#2403
City of Raleigh DMV Ticket		15.00		#2408
VII. CHILDREN OR PARENTS		JULY 15	2k	
City H2O (7-25)	36.68			#2412
CP & L	43.48			#2413
Rent	525.00			#2418
Telephone Bill	25.00			#2487
Miscellaneous	75.00			

g

EDUCATIONAL NEEDS

Listed below are the primary skills one should possess to function successfully in any society. These skills should be mastered by the time one finishes high school and should be taught in all schools.

1. Reading-Writing-Arithmetic

2. Vocational education or career education. (JOB)

3. Common sense

4. An appreciation of different cultures: YOURS and OTHERS.

5. Getting along with others.

6. Self-reliance, Self-discipline

7. A contributing citizen

8. Self-esteem

9. A healthy lifestyle

10. A moral and ethical character

11. An appreciation for art, literature and nature.

12. Being all you can be.

13. Spiritual awareness

h

THE _REAL_ DAILY DOZEN

"S P E M P P-FA R-S I S"

LIFE'S TWELVE DEVELOPMENTAL TASKS

ATTITUDE

What are we talking about?

Webster defines attitude as "a mental feeling or position with regard to a fact or a particular situation." Often you don't have to say a word. People can look at the way you look, the way your head is dropping, the way you're walking, the expression that you wear on your face. And people really won't like to be around you if you've got a bad attitude. Notice the little happy face that made someone millions of dollars; and all they did was use some imagination. They drew a little sunny face and put a little smile on it, and people everywhere bought it and wore it because everybody wants to be liked. And you'll be liked if you have a good attitude.

I have a favorite saying: ***"Attitude determines altitude,"*** which means that the attitude you bring to a situation generally determines how far you're going to go. I think history will bear out the fact that most of the people who have been successful and made good managers weren't the brainiest people in the world; they weren't the richest people in the world, but they were people who got along well with others and were able to use a good attitude to get different groups of people together, organized, and moving on to the next level.

Same talent; different attitudes

I often think about two very successful college basketball coaches I studied religiously – both brilliant but with completely different coaching styles. One has an abrasive attitude - he engenders fear in others. The other commands respect. There's a thin line between fear and respect. I think you should respect people but I don't think you should fear them. In the armed services you have to have fear because on the battlefield if you've got to take a hill, you can't have a democratic discussion about it. You have to follow orders. That's a very good approach if you're going to be a general. But when you're dealing in public service where you can't order people around, you need a different type of attitude to get people to work with you. The former coach I referred to is on a collision course with disaster because of his attitude. It is only a matter of time before he self-destructs.

Start your day off right

Always have a positive mental attitude (I call it **PMA**). When I get up in the morning to go to the bathroom to brush my teeth, I look in the mirror above the face bowl and I say, *"Every day, in every way, I am getting better and better and better."* I repeat that three times as I look at myself in the mirror. Now if you're having trouble looking at that man or woman in the mirror, then some aspect of your life is messed up. You might not know which it is, but if you don't like what you see in that mirror, and you're having problems when you're looking at yourself, then chances are your life elements are out of balance. You want to be able to say, "Every day in every way, I am getting better and better and better." And say it with a

23

smile on your face and believe it. That starts the day off right.

Once you've done that, you always want to think about what happened yesterday and what you're going to do today that's going to make you have a good day. And you're going to iron out those things today that you messed up yesterday, if possible. If you hurt somebody's feelings or if you did something you shouldn't have, you need to call that person or see them and say, " I made a mistake; I was a little tired or a little irritable," and set it straight. They may or may not accept your apology, but you get it off your chest. You can move on from there. You don't have to worry every time you see them crossing the street. You get it cleared out, and then you move on. If they choose to hold onto it, that's their problem, but you get rid of it.

Most people don't start the day the way I just described. They don't think about what they did yesterday. For one thing, most people are going to a job they don't want to go to. That makes it hard to maintain a positive mental attitude.

Parents and grandparents need to start their kids out right so that

24

they'll enjoy starting every day. You want them to be so excited that they can't wait to get up in the morning to go to school. And why are they going to go to school? Because school is going to be enjoyable. And you tell them it's going to be fine; it's going to be fun, and they're shaping themselves to be whatever they want to be. And **whatever they say they want to be, you never tell them they can't be that.**

When a person first starts reading this book and living like this, there's a good chance that they're initially not going to feel as good as they thought they did before. That's what happens when we do a self-examination. This is an x-ray book, and if you do this right, you won't be able to hide from yourself.

The lessons of "MacBasketball"

My basketball coach in college, Coach John McLendon, was a great man and I love him like a father. He was a brilliant man. Coach used to make us play a game called "MacBasketball." He coined that name

25

for a three-on-three, full court game that he invented. It had to be played from baseline to baseline, and on defense you always had to be one arm's length away from your man. You had to guard your player with no help. Coach talked about four degrees of defense. You had to get the ball across the court in five seconds, which meant that there was no rest. If you rested, the other team got a point. And the team that lost had to stay up - until they were just about to drop. He would put a guard on a guard, a forward on a forward, and a center on a center. He would start with the first team, and then go to the second team and the third. Out there on the floor everybody got to see just who were the best players. It was nose to nose. I can tell you that once fatigue sets in and you lose, it ain't no fun. "That's the price you pay for losing," according to the Coach. It was just a game; Coach Mac would just smile. He wouldn't say a thing, but everybody knew. It was the x-ray game because it let everybody in the gym know whether you could play or not. *Fatigue makes cowards of us all.*

That's where I derived my philosophy of basketball: "*94/40, smoke and smother.*" The basketball court is 94 feet long, the game lasts 40 minutes, and during the whole time my teams were expected to keep moving (smoking) and smother the opposing team. Never let up for a minute. Our philosophy was that if we were within ten points in the last six minutes of the game, we were going to beat the other team. We're going to beat them on condition alone, because we were going to be all over them, and they wouldn't be able to jump or run or pass or shoot. We used to beat teams unmercifully, and we wouldn't even be tired at the end of the game. If we were on the road, we'd play another game after that, just among ourselves. That was the kind of shape we were in. We ran 3½ miles every morning before practice, and then we'd run 3½ miles in the evening. And then we would run the steps. We were in terrific shape. That's the way I played in high school and college, and I coached all my teams that way. Everybody knew when we came in, and we packed gyms in high schools and colleges. People came from miles around because it was so exciting. It was non-stop. We called it playing "Simon Pure," which was a reference from my childhood in Clayton, NC. When I was a child, liquor was not available commercially in the county where I lived but there was a lot of "white liquor" (homemade) around. This stuff had no proof on it. It was so strong when you drank it that it almost came out of your ears and nose. The best for miles around was made by a man named Simon. People in that region began to refer to things as "Simon Pure," if they had no imperfections. That's the way our basketball was – Simon Pure.

I still teach youngsters the same way. Today if I conduct a basketball clinic on defense, I'll say, "This is Coach McLendon's four degrees of defense," and then I will take three people or four people out on the court and show them. These days, instead of calling that kind of game "*Simon Pure,*" you're more likely to hear the phrase, "*No shame in my game.*"

A good attitude starts with how you treat your family

When you get up in the morning, make sure you greet everybody in the family with a smile and encourage them to have a good day; ask them how their day is going so far, and tell them you hope everything's going all right. Ask if there's any way you can help them. If you do this, then everybody should leave the house in a pretty good frame of mind. And if not, you can talk about it, either right then or later when there is time. Say, "When we come home this evening we need to sit down and toss this thing around and see what we can do to help the situation."

I tried to do that with my own children, so I didn't have a lot of problems that did not surface with them. When something came up, they said, "Hey Daddy, I think you and I need to talk about some things." So we'd sit down and talk. My wife would join us. Sometimes the girls would want to talk to her, and then she would tell me either directly or indirectly if they didn't want me to know. But there was always an open dialogue, and all the time it was to help everybody to be as pleasant as they possibly could be. I've always said, **"Now don't bring me any doom and gloom."**

Inspiration on the move

After you've told the family goodbye in the morning and you're heading to work or to school, you want to listen to some inspirational, business or educational tapes in the car. There's a lot of road rage out there, so put on your happy face and put on some soothing music, or some positive thinking tapes, or some learning tapes. I have a library of just tapes. And when some aspect of my life is not exactly like it ought to be, I just flip a tape in, and while I drive it will tell me what I need to know. There are tapes available for everything you can imagine - all aspects of your life. I have some meditation tapes that I put on at night, and turn the light off, and they will just take me right on through whatever I want to do. So put on those positive tapes and smile at people on the freeway. Don't give them the finger or dirty looks. If they're honking and glaring at you, just smile and nod and let them think you're a dodo. Reacting any other way just might get you shot these days! Check your pride and show that positive attitude.

Attitude at work

Greet everybody on the job by saying, "Good morning, how are you, how's everything going?" with a little twinkle in your eye; offer a word of encouragement, hum a little tune or something. And keep that same demeanor all day, regardless of whether you really want to jump up and hit somebody in the mouth, because you can't do that. It doesn't help. Pretty soon people will want to be around you. They'll look to you to see what you're doing, and if you're doing your job in a professional manner, they'll see that, and the boss will start inviting you to things. All the time you'll be thinking about where it is you want to go in the organization.

Study those people who are immediately above you so that you can please them first. Find out what they

31

want - not what you want, but what they want - and see if you can make it happen. And once you've figured them out, then think about their bosses. Because once your boss moves up he's got to recommend somebody to move into his place. And if you've been showing a nice attitude, and being a company person, and being helpful, then your boss will recommend that you move up. That's the way you move up the ladder without backstabbing and trying to make somebody else look bad. Never do that. Do your job and treat everybody else well.

There are many books and audiotapes on corporate management and how to get ahead. I gave my son and daughter one on "How To Become CEO." There are seventy-five things that they state as to what to do to become CEO. So put that on in your car on the way to work and listen to it and do the things it says. Find a mentor. Find out what mentors do, and you do it too. That's called mirroring. Do the things that the people you admire and want to be like do.

Bad attitudes

What happens when you encounter people with bad attitudes? Well, first thing you've got to do is try to find out why they have a bad attitude. Is it just today? Is it periodically, or is it constantly? You owe it to them and to yourself to pull them aside at some point, with a smile of course, and say, "You know, it seems like I get on your nerves, or there's something about me, something that I'm doing that seems to upset you. Would you mind telling me what it is?" That takes them off guard. And sometimes it's trivial. But usually there is some reason, and you might not be aware of it. And even when they recall it to you, you might not remember what it was, but then you have to apologize. You have to be bigger than they are, and say, "Well, I really didn't know that. I was not aware. But I think you're a nice person and we're here working together and I have to see you and you have to see me, so let's try to be pleasant to one another and not hurt one another. And if I can help you, fine. Let me know. I'll be willing to help. And I'm glad you told me. And I hope you have a nice day." And move on. If they continue to have a bad attitude toward you, then just try to avoid them because they have some problems.

The value of failure

When I was first coaching I lost a heartbreaking game in Richmond, Virginia. I was young, about 37 years old, and I shouldn't have lost the game, but the fates just got me. The kids did the opposite of the things I told them to do, not because they wanted to, but the pressure got to them. And then with three seconds left, a guy shot a ball that seemed to have no way of going in, but it hit up on the top and fell in. And I lost the game. So we didn't go to the tournament even though we had worked so hard. I was really shaken because it had looked like we were going to get a chance to go.

Tom Harris, who was a legend in coaching at the time, saw it. He liked me because I was young and bodacious, and he came over and dropped his arm on me. He said, "Yeah, you should've won this game.

Fate works like that sometimes. Sometimes you can do all you should do, all the planning you want, and it just doesn't work out. Providence just says, 'Hey, it ain't going to happen.'" He said, "But let me tell you one thing. ***Always let defeat prepare you for your next success.*** I want you to remember that; write that down." I put that up on my wall. I wrote it down on a card, and I put it up right behind my desk. I've had some stinging defeats since then, but I think God was preparing me for roles of leadership at a later point in time. He wanted to let me know how it felt and teach me how to make the most of it.

Unfairness

In addition to failures, I've had people make questionable decisions on more than one occasion, and even sometimes more than once on the same occasion. I couldn't imagine how in the world adult, educated people would do the things that they did. But it showed me that when you're out there dealing with the public - and these were the elite of the elite -

they will do all manner of things to win – things I never would do. In sports, you are playing to see who has prepared the best, and you want everything fair because that's what the rules say. Then for people who are in the education field, of all fields, it just hurt me that they did certain things they shouldn't have done. But there was a voice that said to me, "I'm preparing you for some things down the road, so you will be able to understand them." So it never really bothered me. The funny thing about it was that the crowds from both sides always said, "Man, you won that game. You won that tournament. They just took it from you!" But those things happen, and over the years I've learned that as long as I have a positive mental attitude, and do the best I can, the unfairness does not really bother me; I'm able to get over it and get ready for the next thing. But it's hard to explain to kids. "Keep your head up," you say to them. "We know that people cheated you. That happens."

Leadership and attitude

A positive attitude is essential for a leader who needs to be able to work with other people and encourage them to have positive outlooks too. When you see people with attitudes that are not complimentary to their success, you need to let them know in some subtle way that their problems are probably due to attitude more than anything else. Most people are skilled at what they do - reasonably competent - but it's their attitudes and little idiosyncrasies that keep them from rising above the pettiness. Attitude permeates everything. I've worked in organizations and served on numerous committees, and the biggest problem in getting cooperation between people is their negative attitudes. When it comes to leadership, I believe in **bottoms up, participatory, democratic leadership** - I call it **"BUPDL."**

This approach to leadership applies within the family as well as on the job. In most instances the father is the leader in the household. Not that he knows more than the mother, but if you go back to the natural order of things, the

37

reason that the man became the head of the household is because the wife was going to get pregnant. In an agrarian society, when she was pregnant and had kids, he had to be the person to go out to get things. It didn't mean he was smarter; it didn't mean he was a better leader. It meant that at some point in time the woman was going to be incapacitated, and in order for the household to keep going, society set it up that the man was the household in most instances.

Both partners have responsibility in a household, and if there is a conflict, they need to resolve it objectively. And don't let your ego get the best of you. Often a man doesn't want to go along with something because it's the woman's idea, and women often have the same attitude toward men. We're all supposed to be on the same team. We're supposed to take the best idea, agree on it jointly, and do it. You can never know up front who has the best idea because consequences determine whether it was a good choice. There are going to be consequences, so you just decide which you think is best and deal with

38

it. If it turns out to have been a bad idea, then you just say, "Whoops, that was wrong," without attacking people. Parents really should set a positive attitude atmosphere. But there are times when I think either the father or the mother should bring everybody together and sit down and say, "This family is getting dysfunctional and I think we need to address some things here." That approach applies to organizations beyond the family too. The leader should bring everybody together.

The basic unit of any society is the family. If you can straighten up the families, everything else will be straightened up. Attitude starts first with you – how do you feel about yourself? Then it goes to your family. Then it goes to the people that you don't even know on the highway. Then it goes to the job. Then it goes to other organizations. But in all of those instances, somebody has to take the lead to be able to see and say that some things are out of whack. When you call a meeting, you have the points listed. You have to put them in order of importance – a hierarchy of dysfunctionality. Then you address

39

them by getting everyone's input. And you reach a consensus about what to do to resolve each issue. Then you say, "We've had a good meeting." Everybody has participated.

If a family runs pretty smoothly, then when the children grow up and leave usually they'll take those same traits wherever they go. When I was a boy we used to have family meetings where we would sit around the table and discuss things. Everybody had his say. Everybody. And I think that came about because we used to have family Thanksgiving dinners and Christmas dinners and we would talk about things - family things. It's always been an open family. And there have always been teachers in my family - teachers, preachers and deacons.

Personal accountability

My basic premise is that it's up to the individual to make something out of his or her life. Regardless of your family background, it's up to you. Don't come telling me your troubles - that you were poor, or you didn't have a father or whatever. I hear you, and I'm sorry you didn't have all the advantages, but we are here <u>now</u>. What are we going to do <u>now</u>? What are you going to do today? What are you going to do tomorrow? What's your plan? How do you see yourself? Because **you're responsible for you**.

I have never treated little kids as little kids. Somebody said, "That's why they love you, because you always let them talk." They say, "Little kids and old folks just love you," because I take the time for them. I have a nice personality, and I smile with them, and if you think that won't work just smile at a kid and nod your head at him. He'll come over and play with you. Youngsters have something on their minds too. **There are no blank minds**. It might not be something that their cognitive equipment can handle yet, but there's something on their minds. Ask them, "What is it you want to talk about?" Their thoughts and solutions might not be realistic or even lucid yet, but the thinking is there, and eventually at some time it's going to mature and make sense. The good parent or mentor is able to stay ahead of the curve and can anticipate

41

what the next question will be. Then when it comes, you're prepared with some good answers.

A *daily routine*

When you go to bed at night, give yourself a little time - I usually take thirty minutes - and just relax and think about the day. Praise whatever powers there are for whatever happened that day, the good and the bad. Then think about what you want to do the next day to have another good day. Then sleep well. Go to bed early and get up early. Be discriminating in what you watch on TV. Watch your time, because in my daily activity schedule, there's a six o'clock "get up" time, and a ten o'clock "go to bed" time. And in those hours in between you're either going to be doing something productive or you're going to be asleep.

Anger

I was always supervised and disciplined from an early age. When things came up, I saw how other people handled them. My father was an easygoing man. My uncle was a deacon. My grandfather was a deacon. My great uncle was a preacher. They were lovely people. I saw how they handled things. I didn't see any uncontrolled anger when I was growing up. Even when in athletics, which is a highly passionate endeavor, I've lost championships about which I felt outrage. But I never cursed the officials out. There's a one-liner that says it all for me: **"*If you lose your head, your _ _ _ is sure to follow.*"**

There have been some real hot situations, but usually in those instances you have to walk away. You have to realize where you're going and what you're doing because once you say something that hurts somebody, that's a wound that never heals. I always try to walk away. Well, I try not to let it get to that point. And if I see it going that way, I'll just say, "Well, let's just table this for now, and come back to it later." Usually that will do it.

Of course you don't want to put yourself into situations where there is ongoing tension. You don't want to have a job where you don't like the people you work with or you don't like the boss. It's heck all day. Hopefully by getting in touch with the various aspects of your life you will be able to say in that kind of situation, "You know, I don't think that I'd be doing the company any good by staying here. I don't like it here anymore, and it seems like you don't see things the way I do. I'm going to resign and go somewhere else." Because you've prepared yourself already to go somewhere else. If you're in a personal relationship that is filled with tension, anger or violence, you need to say, "You know, this is not really working out. You have your thoughts about what a relationship should be and I have mine. And it looks like they've gone in different directions. We're just making each other miserable, so I'm going to do you a favor. I'm going to leave. I'm not going to ask you to leave. We'll work out the terms. You know I don't have anything against you, but this is causing me mental anguish and I can't live my life like this, so I'm out of here." Then have somewhere to go and something to do. And then just move on with your life.

Don't let negative things get you down

Former NBA star Magic Johnson spoke to a group of our students shortly after he learned that he had AIDS. We had an AIDS awareness rally at Memorial Auditorium, and he came to St. Augustine's College and spoke. I picked him up at the airport. He said, "Well you know, yeah, I've got this disease. But I've just got to keep on stepping." With his smile and everything, the students really learned the power of positive thinking. Memorial Auditorium was packed. So I sort of picked that up from Magic. Regardless of the situation, *you've got to keep on stepping*.

At the end of this chapter and each succeeding chapter, there will be a few things for you to do in order to have some type of measurable evaluation to guide you in your self-development process.

Please buy yourself a spiral notebook with at least 100 pages for CONFIDENTIAL NOTES. After each chapter, write out your philosophy, feelings, and findings. Do not share them with anyone at anytime. When you finish, study it and update it.

Some things to do.

I.   <u>Attitude</u>:

1. On a scale of 1 - 10 (1 - lowest, 10 highest), how would you rate your attitude at
>   A. Home
>   B. Work
>   C. Place of worship
>   D. Community participation?

2. How do you think your spouse or significant other rates your attitude?

3. How do you think your boss rates your attitude?   Your co-workers?

4. How do you think your children rate your attitude?

5. Write down how you can improve your attitude in all the aforementioned areas.

6. Go to the library. Talk with the librarians. Get on-line. Do research.

7. Find a <u>good</u> <u>COACH.</u>

8. Do what <u>you</u> want to do.

RELATIONSHIPS

What are they?

Webster refers to a relationship as, "The state of being related or interrelated; the state of being mutually interested or involved." My own personal definition is that relationships are the day-to-day involvement that one has with other individuals, groups or a community. My philosophy on relationships is that all relationships should be workable, so that both parties are better off by having the relationship than they would be if it didn't exist. It's what I call *a win-win situation*.

Balance in relationships

Now on any given day you might not feel that way. Feelings will come and go within a relationship until the parties have settled into their comfortable roles. Relationships need to be defined along with what it is that you actually want to receive out of the relationship. Most of the time people want relationships to be skewed in their favor. That's human nature. But at the same time, you don't want to take advantage of other people such that you get more than you take. Most relationships aren't 50/50, but over time there should be a balance that you both can live with.

You should never compromise your integrity in a relationship because, over the long run, the relationship will break down and you will find yourself expressing a lot of anger and rage at some point in the future. Nor should you put anyone else in a situation where they'll have to compromise their own integrity. You have to always control your ego because it will get you into a really big trap. The Bible says, "Pride goeth before a fall." I equate the two - pride and ego - and consider how we're going to look in the eyes of other people. Sometimes you will do things that will be detrimental to you and the relationship and you've got to be very, very careful that you don't fall into what I call the ego trap, or the integrity trap. Because you've got to be able to look at yourself in the morning, and you don't want to look in the mirror and not like that person that you see. If that happens, you're going to be crushed from the inside.

All relationships should make us better people and should help us on our infinite processing route. If they don't, they need to be restructured, if possible.

Family relationships

The first relationship anyone experiences is with the family. You're born into that relationship; you have no choice. When you are young you should feel wanted and loved, and you should be taught those traits that you need to be a good family member. It's up to our parents to make sure that the relationships are good between parent and child and also siblings. Then you have the extended family: the grandparents, uncle, aunts, cousins, etc. Then you move from there to your neighbors, your community. Then you go to your church or your faith organization, your schools, and ultimately your job or profession. All of these relationships should enrich your life and should also make the other person or organization better.

Always contribute as much as you can in a relationship without feeling that you're being taken advantage of. Some people can give more than others. Some people are just genetically geared to be able to give more than others. **Some people are takers; others are givers**. I'm not saying one is better than the other, but you need to know which one you are; and you need to try to give as much as you receive.

I was conditioned to be a giver. I was brought up in an unusual situation in that there was a war going on. My father was fighting in World War II, and I was with my mother. We were both very young, and I had to do the things that needed to be done. So I had to assume a role of significant responsibility and I just figured that was normal. I didn't question it because I didn't know anything else, because my father was not there. Then when my brothers were born, I helped take care of them because they wanted me to and I didn't have any problem with that. So, like many first children, I've been very responsible all my life. I had no problem with it, plus I always had something to give. When I was going to school, the teachers selected the kids that understood what they were doing to help the kids who didn't understand. Nobody had any problems with that. If you didn't understand you asked somebody. I didn't know about everything, but I could ask someone else. We were always sharing, and I think that's the way that it should be.

Teaching and learning relationships

When I started teaching, I quickly found that usually there are three or four levels of students: those who are way out there, those who are not too far out there, those who are average, and those who are below average; and then you have those who probably shouldn't even be in the class. I call those five the A, B, C, D and F groups. Students don't always stay in the same group they start in depending upon their comprehension, but you start them working as a team at an early age. Those who understand the subject become the teachers of those who don't. As the teacher, I set the tone by letting them know that nobody has a cap on all the knowledge. Everybody brings something to the table, so what we're going to do is work together as a team of five. We're going to tackle this problem in the group. Then I would let the groups compete against each other. After some time, they came to love that because everybody loves competition. You earned some extra bonus points if your group won, and then we would switch the groups around. We didn't keep them the same. It was just a marvelous way to teach and to learn. There was a lot of energy in the room.

I think work relationships should be the same way. On the job, you should have managers who are good at the job help the people who are not. The introduction of the "at will" environment in corporate America has been detrimental to on-the-job relationships because now if I help you, you're going to get the job and they'll fire me. In corporations we need to let everybody know that they are valued and that, as long as the numbers are as they should be, there will be no firing or layoffs. And we can't afford to be tight-fisted with compensation. The way to maintain this kind of environment is to have such an effective organization that you out-produce the competition, and everybody shares in the pie. And if, based on business results, the pie is getting smaller, then we try to figure out how we can make it bigger again. This is the type of relationship I like to be in, whether it's at home, in church, on a team, or wherever.

Family reunions

We always had family reunions - big affairs - eighty to a hundred people; and we always had a Christmas dinner in the immediate family. We've sort of kept up that tradition since I was a kid, and I'm sixty-five. One of the things I remember most fondly was the fact that my grandmother made wine. And at Christmas, everybody could drink wine, even the youngsters. We got a little wine too, and that made us feel like we were really a part of the celebration. It was a small demitasse, but we had that; that was our wine. Not only did she make the best wine in the world, but she also made a fruitcake. She started that real early in the season, and she poured wine over it. It was just a great time. And we brought Christmas presents for everybody. Learning about positive, caring relationships starts with the family, and then it goes into the schools.

It's up to the principal to set the tone in school so every kid knows that he's welcome there and the teachers know that they're there to do a job and to help these youngsters become all that they can become. Teachers need to help students understand that they are a school family. Both teachers and students should believe they are going to have the best school, bar none, wherever it is.

When I was growing up, the teachers played with us. We played basketball, volleyball, softball, and we competed; we just had a good time. The teachers we knew were really interested in us as individuals. And they'd whip our butts just as quick as they would smile at us. They weren't whipping us because they didn't like us, and it wasn't brutality or abuse. They did it because they cared. These days, unfortunately, teaching is becoming just a job.

Everybody needs to work (it's a good solution for poverty, boredom and low self-esteem), and relationships in the work community are important parts of our lives. In the work environment there should be an esprit de corps that exists all the way from top to bottom. The same spirit that is engendered in the family should apply to the work community. One of the biggest reasons why we can produce so much in America is because we give a certain amount of democratic freedom to the workers. I think people definitely should be rewarded. Relationships usually are better when there are plenty of resources available for everybody. That way, no one has to think that if they achieve they might be putting someone else at a disadvantage. We need to foster the belief that we all are going to achieve. And although it might not be at the same level, we're going to do everything we can to help each other.

Male/female relationships

There's a lot written and talked about these days concerning the antagonistic relationship between men and woman – they don't understand each other; they speak different languages, etc. I think that's been brought about by the fact that everybody now can be independent or dependent, based on their wishes and their ability to go out and earn. Now that women have the opportunity to earn as much as men (almost, anyway), there is more balance and equality in male/female relationships. There may also be more tension because of this. Women have their own ideas, and their work skills are just as good as men's, which, in some instances, makes men feel threatened. But I like to look at it from an individual standpoint: biologically we're different, but from the standpoint of entering into a relationship we've both got to bring something to the table.

It was my objective to bring up both my sons and my daughters pretty much the same way. Although I realize that there are biological differences, they all had chores to do and we rotated those chores so there was no such thing as a "girl's job" or a "boy's job." Everybody had to wash the dishes and everybody mowed the grass. If the girls' curfew was 12:00, the boys' was 12:00 too. When you raise children in a way in which they can play all roles, they learn to have a greater appreciation for both genders. Then when they grow up they don't suffer from old-fashioned gender stereotype thinking.

Relationships with our children

In entering into an intimate relationship, each of us needs to think carefully about the question of bringing children into the world. Before making the decision to have a child, or to run the risk of having an unplanned child, we need to have thought through how we will take care of that person. In the classes I taught where we dealt with intimate relationships and sexuality, I did not let the females take only the female point of view. They had to be the males too; and the males had to think like females. If you were a male, I made you approach the problem and defend the problem from the female point of view. And whoever won the debate won the debate. And there were some interesting outcomes to this teaching approach. We found out that males had a male psyche about things, and females had a female psyche about things. But when they had to reverse them and put themselves in the opposite position, it gave them a deeper insight into things.

In my college classes, most of the guys wanted to have their careers and they wanted their wives to stay home and take care of the children. Well we found out that the females wanted to work too. But there was a fact that you couldn't get around: if you're going to have children, somebody's going to have to take care of them. Now who's going to do it? And are you going to be making a lot of money? So what are the chores that you want to do; what are the chores that you don't want to do? And we found out, over a period of years, that nobody really wanted to do the dirty work. The males didn't want to do it and neither did the females. They wanted to do the things that were glamorous. They did not want to stay home and take care of the children.

My own philosophy on childrearing

I believe that the first few years of marriage should be spent planning the rest of your life together. You shouldn't have children until either the wife or the husband can stay home with the children for their first three years. The first three years of a child's life are a critical development period, and I don't think it starts after a baby's born. Once a couple decides to have a child, I think the wife should stop working, or she shouldn't go past the point where work is going to create stress. I think those three years are the most important three years of a child's life and that both parents need to sacrifice in order to make sure the child's life starts off on the right foot.

I know this is a controversial position these days and, like everything else in this book, I offer it up for consideration only. Each individual must make his or her own decisions about how to live their lives. However, in a marriage, a couple should discuss these subjects and reach a mutually agreeable decision on how to handle the responsibility of raising children. This obviously links to managing the financial aspects of your life, which is discussed in a later chapter. Your finances should be in shape such that somebody can stay home with the children for three years. This is an ideal situation, in my opinion. Or if both parents have to work, one should take on work that does not take a lot of time away from the children. This is the period in which parents need to be trying to gear their youngsters for life.

Before you have children, you have to develop a philosophy of parenting and having children. And when you have them you should be in it for life.

My definition of a parent is someone who's willing to take care of somebody for the rest of their life if need be. We always assume that our children will be healthy and when they're 18 or 21, they'll be grown up and on their own, but that doesn't always happen. If you bring children into the world you have to be able to support them if necessary for as long as they live. Many people don't think about that. If they have a kid who is ill equipped to deal with the world, then what are they going to do? When you get ready you've got to first think, "This is my child for life."

Parenting is a relationship for life.

If you're going to bring kids into the world, hopefully you will choose a mate who will complement what you can give them, inasmuch as the children are going to have to live the rest of their lives with the genes you give them. You don't want to bring a child into the world who's going to be at a disadvantage if you can avoid it. Now that kind of thinking is going to create some problems for some people. Some people will say they don't think it's right to consider such things. I'm just letting you know that you could create problems for yourself and for your children, so don't be surprised. Don't say you didn't know. This is the purpose of the relationship.

There are many famous books on parenting, and you need to get a grasp of how to take care and raise a baby before you actually have one. Biologically speaking, after the end of four years, a baby will have developed most of his or her personality traits. Then it's just a matter of training. I think the mother is best equipped to do that, and the father gives the male side of it when he comes home to supplement whatever needs to be done. After that, you raise them together. But I think primarily that is the way that nature prepared us to raise children. And after the kids are older, if the mother wants to go back to work and you're able to do it financially, she should go back to whatever she needs or wants to do. But give the kids the best training that you can afford. Sacrifice!!

There's going to be strain on the intimate part of the marriage relationship when there's so much focus on raising children. So the couple needs to make sure and find the time to be intimate with each other. They will both be busy during the day, so the time that they're going to have is in the evenings, or on weekends. I was fortunate to have a job that everybody enjoyed doing.

We went to the ball games and other activities as a family. The kids went with us. Even when they were babies, we put them in pasteboard boxes and carried them with us and the fans would hold them in the boxes. So they were socialized that way. We never really had problems finding ways to spend time together. Later, we were able to put them in good kindergartens and our relationship didn't suffer. Neither did the kids suffer. Now I realize that was an ideal situation.

The marriage relationship

Communication is very important for a couple in order to keep their marriage healthy. They need to sit down and discuss problems before they internalize them and then all of a sudden they erupt, and then one person says, "Well I didn't know that you felt that way." You need to air all those problems that exist, not every day, but if you see that habits are starting to form you need to be able to sit down with your spouse and say, " I think we need to talk about this," not in order to blame or accuse but just to say, "How do you think we need to resolve this? This is how I feel. How do you feel?" And if you love each other, you'll come to some pretty good conclusions. I think the best way to have a male/female relationship, if you want to have kids, is to be married. And the reason for that is, once you're married, you're making a commitment. And you're making a commitment hopefully for life, but it might not last for life. You want to make a relationship for as long as you think you need to make it. But if you want to have kids, you want to make it for at least a long time such that the kids don't suffer. Marriage makes one take a commitment. It makes one think about things. It lets the public know what your thoughts are. Plus it protects the children and particularly the mother, because you have a legal entity to make sure that the mother and children are financially taken care of in case things don't work out down the road. If your spouse says, "I don't think I like this any more, and I think I'm going to leave," then you're left out there. It's best to have the relationship supported legally in terms of protecting your property rights. Some people like cohabitation; many people do it. It might be an okay lifestyle for the very rich or the very poor – in the former case, one can pay for whatever might come up at a later time, and in the latter, one doesn't have anything, so it doesn't really matter – but for the majority of people, I think marriage is best.

If your marriage doesn't last

Over a period of years, people change, situations change, and many relationships don't last. Nature does not create a union called marriage. Marriage is a creation of human beings. Biologically, at the end of four years, the giddy-like passion or fiery, intimate relationship that existed between two people fades. This is because nature equipped men, to make sure that the species survived, to have many partners so that the genetic material would be spread around for an improved species. Therefore, if one relationship did not produce offspring, then another one would. So, from the standpoint of nature, the love relationship is going to be redefined over time. But there are a lot of different types and degrees of love, and you cannot endure the type of emotional highs and physiological expressions that passion is going to put on you forever because the intensity is very great and you would be unable to proceed upward in your relationship.

If the marriage doesn't last and there is a divorce, there still should be the type of relationship between the two people that is in the best interests of the children. This is true, regardless of how or why the divorce might have come about. It takes a pretty big person to be able get past hurt and anger, but you should have the best interests of the other person and the children at heart.

Alternative lifestyles and relationships

Society has developed some norms and rules over time that work best for civilization in general. But things that work best for civilization and society are not always best for the individual. No one should stay in a relationship that is detrimental to his or her health: physical, mental or emotional. But we don't really know what lifestyles are best for other people. We can only say what lifestyle is best for us. And although there are lifestyles that are outside the norm or are not what society would like them to be, they're not dangerous or threatening to the rest of the world. Relationships should not only be in the best interests of all the parties involved, but they should not be detrimental to other people. If a relationship meets that test, then why not be in it? It's simply a matter of choice. *GOD DID NOT GIVE US ANSWERS; HE GAVE US CHOICES.*

Some things for you to do in your personal notebook.

II. <u>RELATIONSHIPS:</u>

A. *On a scale of 1 - 10, how would you rate your Relationship with*

1. *Your spouse or significant other*

2. *Your boss*

3. *Your co-workers*

4. *Your children*

5. *Your family members*

6. *People of different races?*

7. *What relationships do you need to improve?*

8. *Write out your plans for improving relationships.*

9. *Give a copy of this book to a member of another race that you think could use it. Discuss it with the person over lunch. Invite him or her for dinner.*

10. *Go to the library. Talk with the librarians. Go on-line. Do research.*

11. *Find a <u>good</u> <u>COACH</u>.*

12. *Do what <u>you</u> want to do.*

IMAGINATION

What is it?

    Imagination is the basis of all creation: the ability to think and fantasize without limits. Webster defines imagination as "the act of forming a mental image of something not present to the senses, or not previously known or experienced." My thoughts are that everything started with imagination. God had to have an imagination; and out of His imagination came some thoughts, and out of these thoughts, He was able to create His thoughts through words, then deeds. Creation usually starts with a perception or thought, then a word or words and then deeds or actions, so I think of imagination as the beginning of the creative process. Thoughts bombard our minds all day. The brain is never vacant. There's always something on the mind. According to research, between forty and eighty thousand thoughts come into our minds in the course of a twenty-four-hour period. If you think about it, there's never any time when your mind is blank. There's always something up there; and it goes very fast. It's always happening, regardless of whatever else you're doing.

I'm talking about imagination without limits, and imagination pervades all of the aspects of our lives. How can you imagine how healthy you can be? How can you imagine how financially sound you can be? There are not limits. Try thinking and imagining without any limits or boundaries. Through a process called creative visualization and verbal affirmations you can literally create your future. If you can visually imagine or see where you want to go, and if you can tell yourself over and over how it's going to be, those are two ways in which you can do things. It's been proven that you can learn how to hit a golf ball better just by sitting back and visualizing the perfect golf swing and how you do it. Verbal affirmation means that after you see yourself doing something, you say out loud what you've done, and you can actually see yourself doing it. Praise and congratulate yourself on the accomplishment. ***BE what you intend to be. BEHAVE as if you already ARE.***

How to turn random ideas into realities

Everything in this world was created. It all came from thought and imagination. So in order to tap into your imagination and let it work for you, you need to **open your mind** to all the thoughts running through it. Once these thoughts are bombarding your mind, imaginations will run rampant. There will be some that will interest you more than others, and those you will want to pursue to **the next step: fantasizing.** After you've imagined something, then fantasize about how far you can take it. You do this without imposing any limits on your imagination. The difference between imagining and fantasizing is that fantasizing is a more active focusing in your mind about how big an idea could be. In the imagination phase, the idea just floats into your mind.

I personally believe that all thoughts go to and come from a supernatural realm - a spiritual world. I think everything that's ever been thought or ever will be thought is out there, and it's up to us to be able to tap into it, and retrieve those thoughts. When I say you need to fantasize "without limits," I mean that if you catch yourself thinking that something's not possible, or that it can't happen, you have to stop yourself. Open back up.

Once you get through the fantasy phase, then you **think about the possibilities**. You introduce a little bit of reality to the picture. What's possible is usually dictated by the availability of resources, including people. After you have explored the possibilities around an idea, you then **focus on the probabilities**. Then you establish some hypotheses, which are selected solutions that you think that you can use at that particular point in time. After you assess the probabilities of an idea, you'll find that you don't have all the resources you need; you don't have all the knowledge; you don't have all the people, etc. But within that imagined thought, you have found something tangible that you want to do and you believe is possible and probable. Now you have moved from unlimited thoughts to pragmatic possibilities. Then you have to choose one or two of these possibilities that you think you can actually pull off to create whatever it is that you want to create.

Now here comes the challenge: you have to do the research. You have to find out what is and what isn't. After you have researched the literature and talked to the experts, then you need to form an opinion as to how you think it will work for you. This could involve either improving on something that already exists, or creating something that has never existed. Once you develop your information base, you will know where to go. At this stage, you need to **write your plan down in detail**. You don't have to do this by yourself: you can get as many people involved with you as is necessary. You can form what I call an **"ENTERGY,"** that is a team-based energy effort. If you consider corporations and venture capitalists, all of them started with an idea and imagination, and then they persuaded other people that their ideas were good. Henry Ford imagined a world with cars; scientists fantasized about television; Bill Gates and his colleagues imagined life with Microsoft software, etc. All of those ideas were elements of imagination first, and then they became realities. But those visionaries had to get other people to believe - bankers, research people, engineers, etc. - and they formed "ENTERGY" teams to bring their ideas to fruition. Your detailed plan needs to include a detailed time line as well. I like to manage by objectives (MBO), that is, break all tasks down into small manageable units connected with time deadlines. This enables you to measure or evaluate your rate of success. It keeps you moving toward your predetermined goals. Pharmaceutical companies like Glaxo Wellcome imagine that it is possible to create drugs to cure any number of diseases. They know those cures are out there, but they haven't found all of them yet. All of the ideas that come out of these imaginings will not be successful, but failure in itself is not failure, it just eliminates some of the possibilities. We use this process - the "trial and error" method - to guide us toward success.

Now we cannot force things to be. We don't want to fool ourselves and disregard reality just to reach what we want to reach. If we find that the research and the experimentation do not point in the direction we want to go, we can't try to force it. Many people are so convinced that something should happen that they try for it over and over again. Someone defined insanity as doing the same thing over and over and expecting a different result. You must be able to discard ideas if they do not work out.

The Million Family March

I went to the Million Family March in Washington, D.C., in 2000 and it was a lovely event. There were families of all types from all over who had come to look for answers to the issues of life as a family. On Sunday of the same weekend there was the Million Women's March. There were females from 157 countries. There were women of all lifestyles and persuasions from all parts of the world discussing some of the terrible abuses that occur against women in some underdeveloped and developed nations as well as some injustices that happen in America. There was discussion of gender prejudice, class prejudice and racial prejudice. The theme was that you have to get rid of all of the prejudices in the world because all of us are God's children, and everybody has basic rights as a human being, and that's what America's all about. It was a wonderful conference, and the most important message I got out of it was *if things are going to change it's going to have to be the people who change them*. When you're trying to resolve any type of problem, everybody has to leave the table with something. The rich have a mind set that is rational to them. The poor people have a rationale that is viable to them. So what are the things that we can get together on? First, we can say that everybody has a right to certain things, and then you go from there. But a guy who's paying a lot of taxes does not necessarily want that money to go to other people. On the flip side, the person who doesn't have much gets ticked off seeing people having thousand dollar parties. Somebody has to be able to have the rich and the poor together come up with some type of workable plan. I think that can be done. I think it must be done. I don't know who that person is, but it seems that everybody at the Million Family March was receptive to the idea.

Cooperative Competition

In a process I call "cooperative competition," everybody tries to do the best that he or she can. Naturally there are always some losers - people who do not reach the top — but they are helped by the people who do get to the top. And it just keeps going and going, and that makes the pie bigger and bigger. All you need is imagination and the ability to sit down and see what everybody needs, and then debate those issues rationally. Once you get **the basic needs** of everybody met, then you can use your remaining energy to pursue people's wants. I think everybody should be rich. I think everybody should aspire to be rich, because I've found that rich people do a lot of things to help other people in literature, architecture, philanthropy and many other areas as well. I think rich people are great. I think poor people are great. I think that once you have a lot of money you should use some of that money to help other people who have needs. Not necessarily individual donations, but put something into your legacy that will enable other people to move up. That's the way I try to live my life. I don't have a lot of money but I do give to a lot of charities, colleges and individuals. I try to do a lot of things to help others. I sit on a lot of boards. I enjoy doing that because I think that's what the situation needs. *To whom much is given, much is expected.*

Everything comes from imagination.

There can be no progress without imagination. There can be no creativity without imagination. It fuels everything. Many things that we take for granted now would have been laughed off as crazy ideas a hundred years ago. The telephone? Television? Satellite communication? So someone's idea today might sound crazy to us, but that believer thinks it can be done. I don't think that there is anything that is impossible. I know we have physical laws and natural laws, but there are ways to get around them too. ***Anything's possible.***

"Edu-car-letics"

You can be whatever you want to be. Many young people come to college without any idea about what they want to do. They have never even thought about it. The question has never gotten to them. One of the first assignments I gave my new students was to write a one-page autobiography and to include in it their goals, where they were going to go, and what they were doing to achieve their ambitions. That exercise made them focus. I am creating an organization now that works with young people to ***focus on education, careers and athletics*** combined into one word. It's called *"**Educarletics.**"* All the youngsters in it know that they are in a basketball program that I assist with the youth basketball leagues in the city of Raleigh, NC. Currently we work with ages 10 to 13. We have little leagues, and through basketball these youngsters learn critical life skills. Athletics is a very educational endeavor. First of all, it teaches you how to work with a team, with other people; you all have several basic goals wrapped around one common goal, **which is to win**. So it teaches you how to be a team player. Secondly, it teaches you the rules of the game: that no matter what types of games you're in, there are certain rules and strategies that you have to obey. The third thing it teaches you is that in order to win you have to work as hard as you possibly can. You must focus on what you are doing. The fourth lesson is you must be in shape in order to play the game. Finally, then five, you've got to play as smart as you can. That means getting an education. You've got to be smart about the game, and those are the five lessons of Educarletics. We're teaching them that they not only have to play **athletics** this way, but in **education** and **career planning** they have to do the same thing. In order to play, in order to get to the pros, they have to go through school. Most of them do not have enough money to go to school on their own, so they have to get a scholarship. There are schools everywhere, and if a young person stays in our program and follows this plan, he or she stands a good chance of getting into a college or a junior college somewhere, through either athletic or academic ability. Some of them have great skills; I can tell that some of them are going to be great basketball players if they stay focused. Some of them know about the pro experience because their parents play or have played in college and in the NBA, and other kids are going to learn about it from them. "Educarletics" is going to prepare these kids for an **education** and for a **career** - a professional athletic career, if that's what they want because, although they come to play basketball, we also have computers and other learning resources available, and we **include the whole family - parents, grandparents, everybody. Everybody plays**: parents, grandparents, uncles, aunts and interested neighbors. And then we eat hot dogs and hamburgers. We go on outings like camping trips and we have tournaments on the weekends with 25 or 30 teams invited from all over the area. We also invite people in to speak to the kids about certain things of importance in making them productive citizens. Those that want to play golf can use Meadowbrook County Club, which is a Black country club in Raleigh, NC. Most people really don't know about Meadowbrook, which was built in 1958. We couldn't go to the white folks' clubs, so we built one for ourselves: tennis courts, swimming pool, everything. We didn't let our imagination stop us from doing it. We just asked ourselves what we needed to do to get it done? And then we just went on and did it. You can do a lot of things if you just imagine you can do them, which is closely tied to your attitude. You can use imagination as a positive tool to get whatever you want, and imagination goes through all of the various aspects of our lives – *IMAGINATION AND ATTITUDE*.

Creativity follows a passion.

There is *imagination,* there's *passion*, and then there's *creativity.* Passion is a love for doing what it is you're doing, regardless of the monetary reward. Some people just enjoy doing what they're doing. I never felt like I worked a day in my life because I love coaching and teaching. It was great that I happened to be paid well for it, but had I not been paid well, I would have done it anyway. If you have a passion for something and you do it well, you're going to get paid because you're going to get better and better, and your product or service is going to be in greater and greater demand. You don't have to put any limits on your thinking because you know it's always an infinite process. So no matter if you come out undefeated, you know that the game still needs to be taken to another level. You're never there. You're always in the process of getting there. And you've got to continually do better and better. That's only if you have the passion. And once the passion to go to higher level leaves you, be comfortable where you are. To go further without passion might lead you to incompetence.

Aspire to be successful (in some hierarchical pattern that includes spirituality, health, knowledge, wisdom, wealth and fame).

Unfortunately, the vast majority of people aren't lucky enough to have found the thing that they're passionate about, so they're still trying to figure out how to do that. They get caught up in whatever it takes to make a living, and sometimes that squeezes out the time for the thing that they're passionate about.

People think about making a living. People should be thinking about making a fortune. And then in the process you'll make a living. That might seem a little funny, but most people say, "Oh, if I could make a living." You want to make a fortune. Make a fortune in what it is you do. If Tiger Woods can make a hundred million dollars hitting the golf ball, I know you can find something that you enjoy doing. Can you just imagine? It's almost insane when you think of it that someone can make a hundred million dollars in a few years just hitting a golf ball. So he's not making a living, although there are a lot of golfers that are playing who are just putting bread on the table.

A book for all families

I thought about all this when I saw the Million Family March and all the things that the families were looking for. They seemed to seek a definitive direction. They were all looking for guidance and some help in finding the answers to their problems. It helped put this project in a bigger perspective. It made me see that the ideas I'm putting forth here are designed to help all families everywhere: rich, poor, black, white, yellow, brown, wired or unwired.

Some things to do.

III.   **_IMAGINATION:_**

1. Can you imagine yourself outside-the-box?

2. Fantasize on what you would imagine yourself to be without any limitations.

3. Write out what you have a passion to
do and your plan for achieving it.

4. Go to the library. Talk with the librarians. Get on-line. Do research.

5. Find a _good_ _COACH_.

6. Do what _you_ want to do!

SOCIALIZING

Define it first

Webster defines sociality as "pleasant companionships with one's friends and acquaintances; friendly relationships with others". My philosophy is that you should be sociable and social with everybody, unless you run into some things that would be detrimental to you, the other person or the organization. I think first of all you have to be sociable with yourself. It's very difficult to be social with someone else if you don't get along with yourself. Now that seems crazy, but what do I mean? I discovered early that **if you're going to be happy it's left up to you, not anybody else.** Often, people think things – belonging to the right cliques, going to the best clubs, wearing the right clothes, being invited to certain events - are what makes you a person and what makes you happy. I don't think so. I think basically, deep down within, you have to be satisfied with yourself first, and you should be able to be social with yourself, and practice enjoying yourself with yourself as much as possible.

Socializing with yourself

I sometimes celebrate what I call *"ME"* days and throw *"ME PARTIES"*. My wife does the same thing. That means that **today is my day. It's for me.** It's going to be designed by me for me. I'm going to have a good time with me. Sometimes you get caught up in the stresses of work, the family, taking care of everybody else's business but yours, you feel uptight and you need to unwind and do some things for you. That's when you should decide that it's time to just take this day and use it as you see fit. A "ME DAY" is usually pretty unstructured; it's just **whatever you want to do that day.** I like to read and listen to good music, and I like to play golf, and sometimes I just like to walk the malls. Wherever my passions lead me for that day, that's what I do. I tell people this is a "ME DAY." I say, "Need a little space today." Don't ask me to mow the lawn. Don't ask me to do a thing. **I'm going** *to do whatever I want to do today*, because I need to unwind.

Set the right tone with your children

Basically, we are social beings. We belong to and feel secure in groups. The natural order of things says that we grew up living in a communal type atmosphere. Most of the social habits that we get come from first the family, then from the neighborhood and our friends and so on. So how we socialize our children in relationships with us goes a long way in determining how they're going to react with other people. If we're uptight and "anti" and don't socialize well, or don't have what we call a pleasant personality (which we dealt with in the chapter on attitudes), chances are our kids are going to be the same way. So sociality really begins in the home, and in the family, and then the neighborhoods. We don't need the Hatfields and the McCoys any more.

More about "Edu-car-letics"

The "Educarletics" program I spoke about in the chapter on Imagination mainly focuses on the African American community because most African American males like playing basketball. It is the cities' game. I don't know whether it's because we've lived primarily in the inner cities, and by nature, living in the inner city means that you have to get along with your neighbor or what, but there are a lot of good role models right there, and they don't necessarily have to be professional ball players. There are former players in the community whom the kids look up to and respect. So what we try to do is get them together and form a league that plays in different areas. I give clinics to kids as young as seven and as old as eighteen. We stress how to behave like gentlemen, how to play with your team, how to get along with your teammates; this is family. What we've found out is that once kids start playing together they learn about how to behave in a group environment; they watch you very, very closely to see how you react. They watch to see if you have favorites - if a kid is playing because his daddy donates the money to the Y, for example. We try to treat them all the same. We take them on outings to different places. We talk about being sociable, having a nice attitude. We try to create a model, a positive model, outside the home if there's not one in the home because *this learning must happen at an early age.*

"Intergenerational Collaborative Entergy"

As I have said earlier in this book, there is another program, called *"ICE"* - that's *"Intergenerational Collaborative Entergy,"* in which we try to involve everyone that a kid interacts with. We hold social events to which we invite not only the kids but also their parents and their grandparents, and any other significant others. Because they like to play basketball, our motto is, *"If not the NBA, then as far as you can go."* That tells people that we want excellence, and all of the attributes that go along with it. When the kids are playing and having a good time, and when you eat and drink together, the parents have a tendency to meet and greet each other too. And then we get a chance to tell them about the things that we're trying to do with the youngsters. Basically, there are five lessons to learn on the court: (1) We want them to play together. (2) We want them to play fair. (3) We want them to play hard. (4) We want them to play smart. (5) We want them to play at increasing skill levels. We also want them to get their education. We want them to have a spiritual awareness and know that there are inner resources within themselves that they can turn to when others don't understand their situations. Those are the values we try to instill. When we have tournaments on Saturdays or weekends with different groups and their parents, we have hot dogs and hamburgers, and sometimes we got out to somewhere like the pizza parlors. We don't place a lot of emphasis on who won or who lost. You had a good time. You played hard. You did the best you could. So to us that's what success is. We try to put these leagues in the faith communities also. It works very well in the Sunday schools and other youth development programs, and more churches are using athletics as a way of bringing youngsters into the church. In some of the churches we have computers, and we rotate the teams in and out to give the kids exposure to computers. We'll be teaching career skills in one hour while the others are playing basketball and still others are on computers. The next objective is to go to schools and get the teachers in on this. I think you've got to integrate and cooperate with all the generations. *Everybody's got to work together as an "ICE"-team.* The more people you involve the better off it will be. And then you get to colleges. You have the lettermen clubs, sororities, and fraternities, and since the '60's, the social fellowship groups. Social fellowship groups were developed for those kids whose parents didn't have the money it often takes to get into the sororities or fraternities, or they didn't have the GPA, but wanted to have a group to which they could belong. Because everybody wants to feel like they belong.

The need to belong

In Maslow's Hierarchy of Needs, about third up on the hierarchy, is the need to belong. That's why we have gangs, because they want to belong to something. There's nothing wrong with gangs as long as those gangs are taught the things that they need to do to be productive. People usually assume a bad definition of what a gang is, but all it is is a group of people who do similar things, who enjoy each other's company. As adults, we have to be able to see who the gang members are, try to get them to communicate with us and then teach them positive things, rather than say, "Well, they're bad guys." They're bad guys because nobody has taken the time to sit down with them and ask them, "Hey, what is it that you guys want to do? Let's see what we can do constructively so that you can live a long and productive life." We welcome gangs. We talk to the people that might be in the gangs, and we try to do a positive turnaround rather than being fearful of them. We include them in forums and talk and embrace them also.

Socializing at home

I recently had a big birthday party where there were people from all over the world. It was an international party. My wife is a great entertainer and she put some snacks out on the deck; the food was in the dining room. We always have videotapes playing of various musical artists. We had Whitney Houston's latest video in the sitting room upstairs. Downstairs, we had the football game on for the guys who wanted to watch it. We had some little snacks in that room, and in the other den, my computer room, we had the beverages. The reason for spreading everything around the house was that it required everybody to move around and not stay in one place. If you don't do that, they'll get into a little pocket. When you put things in different places, they have to mingle to get them, and then they talk, introduce themselves, and everybody just has a great time. This approach to social gatherings can be used in school, church, job, wherever. But you need to know who your people are because you want to make sure you have a good cross section. At my party, everybody had a chance to mingle, and there were some very interesting conversations going on. It was also designed so that people couldn't just sit down in one area. I always rent extra chairs, but I didn't put enough chairs out to start with on purpose because I wanted people to stand up, mingle and walk around looking for an empty chair. After they had stood there for a little while I would ask them, "Do you need a chair?" and I would get them one. I had forty folding chairs outside in my van, but I took them out as I needed them so that when new people walked in they initially didn't have a chair. They had to walk and hunt. We ultimately used all forty chairs, but I mixed the crowd up and encouraged conversation by parceling them out over the length of the party. That's an example of what I mean about being social.

Socializing across ethnic groups

I make a point of socializing with different races and ethnic groups regularly. Whether they are white, Latin, Asian or Hispanic, I like to go to their events and just walk around and meet friends and smile. Sometimes they get a little amazed and confused as to why I'm there, but that doesn't matter to me. I meet new people, have a lot of fun, and life doesn't become boring. I tell my wife, "Well, we're going to be Mexican tonight," or, "We're doing country and western tonight." The people usually will become friendly if you're friendly. I tell them, "Well this is the first time I've been here and can you teach me how to do this?" Or I watch the room to see who's amiable and who smiles and waves and seems approachable. If somebody has an attitude, I definitely do not ask that person for any kind of assistance. I've found that most of the time they're curious and want to know who you are and why you came. By doing this it helps me understand how other people feel, how they do things, and then I can invite them to my affairs too. I always carry my personal business cards in my pocket. I have several different business cards. I give them one and say, "Give me a ring if I can help you."

Sociability on the job

Being sociable on the job means getting along with your co-workers. Since most businesses are focused on bottom line and quarterly results, I think there should be some type of social gathering for employees at the end of the quarter to let them know that what they are doing is appreciated and how it can be improved upon. The company may or may not have reached its targets. If they did reach them, well good; they can have a great party. If they fell short, then they can discuss how to do better next quarter. Recognizing that morale might be down a little bit, management could explain the reasons they didn't get to the goal. They should reinforce the fact that they're a team and that they're going to have this social or family gathering regardless of the bottom line. I think **a corporation that** *plays together prospers together*, and I think the CEO should be there along with his or her managers, and they should just have a good family time. At that same time management can get all the team together, when everybody's feeling good, and let them know where you are, what you're doing, and what your prospects are for the next quarter. The managers should recognize the contributions of their staff and ask them to stand up and be recognized. They should also share what the projections are for the next quarter and engage the team in discussing ways to insure that they make their targets. This kind of ritual is important for team spirit because, although people work together, they often don't socialize together. And once they have a chance to socialize together they find out that they're basically all the same.

What kind of day do you want it to be?

It's a beautiful day if you decide it is. I read the newspapers on the weekends because they have the listings of what's going on in the area, and we just arbitrarily pick something that we want to do, and just go. It's just beautiful.

So basically what I'm trying to say in a nutshell is that **it's left up to you to decide how sociable you're going to be and how you're going to relate with others**. You go to them. Don't look for them to come to you. You always have to take the initiative to do anything if you want to enjoy life. Don't ever look to anybody else to try to make things happen for you. You have to make them happen.

God doesn't make bad days. I don't have bad days. And I counsel people trying to bring bad days to me.

Some things to do.

IV. **SOCIALIZING:**

1. How would you describe yourself socially -- shy or outgoing?

2. How do you fit in social gatherings?

3. What would you like to improve socially?

4. How do you feel in racially diverse social settings?

5. Write out how you can improve socially.

6. Go to the library. Talk with the librarians. Get on-line. Do research.

7. Find a _good_ _COACH_.

8. Do what _you_ want to do!

EDUCATION

What is it?

Webster defines education as "the action or process of educating or being educated; a field of study dealing with the methods of teaching and learning; to provide someone with schooling; to develop mentally and morally; to provide information; to instruct, teach." One of the school superintendents with whom I worked told me that his definition of education was "teachers teaching and students learning". I personally prefer a little broader definition: I believe education is *the ability to do what is needed when it needs to be done, whether you want to or not*. And it can be in either a formal or an informal setting. It's finding out the specific skills that are needed to perform a certain task, developing them, and *CHANGING YOUR BEHAVIOR*. I don't think you can be truly educated if your behavior doesn't change. When I was teaching health classes, we would do a self-inventory. Some of the students smoked. After we had completed the textbook chapter on smoking, I would expect that if the students had understood the ramifications of smoking, they would know that smoking was not good for them. If they hadn't quit smoking by the time the semester ended, I didn't know whether they had been educated or not. I put much more emphasis on "how is your behavior?" than on "what do you know?"

Infinite Processing

My philosophy of living is, "***Every day, in every way, I am getting better and better and better.***" We can never stop learning – educating ourselves. Living is a lifelong learning process; a journey, not a destination. Enjoy the journey.

Bloom's Taxonomy of Learning

Bloom classified learning into six parameters. The first is **Memory**: you have to be able to memorize information in order to go on to the next step, which is **Comprehension**. After you have memorized it, can you comprehend what it means? The next level in Bloom's Taxonomy is can you use the information? Is it **Applicable**? Then comes **Analysis**: can you take the information apart to see how it is put together. Next comes **Synthesis**, which I believe is the most important step because now you're creating. You've taken something that you've learned and you've used. You've taken it apart and now you're going to take it to another level: you're going to create something better or new out of it. For example, first there was the typewriter, then came the telegraph, the computer, the Internet, and everything has continued to improve over time. Now we have computers and second and third generation memories, etc. This is what Bloom was talking about. The last step in Bloom's Taxonomy is **Evaluating**. Can you **judge** whether it was good or bad, or whether it was neutral in its effect on the larger community, not necessarily you. I've added a seventh step, which I say is **Refining**, and that means you're getting better and better and better in creating a better you and a better society. You are increasingly being able to make the people around you better.

Lifelong learning

It's a beautiful thing when you talk to youngsters, or anyone, about lifelong learning. It never stops. There's always something you're interested in – not the same thing all the time; eventually you'd get bored with that. But when you look at the different parameters of something, it makes life exciting and enjoyable because when you go to bed at night and you're analyzing your day. You say, "Tomorrow I think I'll learn about this or I'll do that." It's really an exciting way to live life because there's always something new out there, and you're getting an education at the same time. Once again, the setting doesn't have to be a formal one. You can learn wherever you are. *All the world is a classroom.*

Making time for education

Regardless of whether it's formal or informal, there are 168 hours in each week for everybody all over the world. What you do to educate yourself in those 168 hours, whether it's on the job, in a sport, or in the classroom, you have to determine how you're going to use your time to get educated. (See Daily Activity Schedule attached.) Given the fact that we all have to sleep, I normally think of the day as being from 6:00 a.m. to 11:00 p.m. That's the general time frame we have to work with. Normally in America the workday starts anywhere from 7:00 to 9:00 in the morning, and you generally work an eight-hour day. Of course self-employed people may not have this kind of predictable and controllable schedule. If you're going to fit education into that limited time frame, you're going to have to have a certain time that you have to get up, do your grooming and get to the job or wherever you need to go. During the hours that are available to you for learning, you have to decide what you really want to do. _Use_ your discretionary time wisely and to your development.

Your Daily Activities Schedule

At the beginning of every semester in every class I taught, I had the students write their autobiographies. This was a way to find out who they were and to tell them who I was. I wanted to hear from them about their plans. They were there to get an education, and I knew from experience that most people did not manage their time effectively. In order to educate them about time management, I gave them each a form to fill out every week for the first 30 days of the class - their **DAILY ACTIVITIES SCHEDULE**. At the end of each week I would take them up and review them.

They would fill in their class schedules and when they were going to study for each class. It's usually a good idea to study right after a class because the material is on your mind. I would tell them I was programming them to make A's in all their classes. I would say, "Right now you have an A in my class. If you follow your Daily Activity Schedule, do what you're supposed to do, and turn in your assignments, then you've got a roadmap for how to be an A student. I explained why they were required to review their schedules every week for the first month because it forced them to look back and see what they hadn't gotten done. "You'll get behind," I'd say, "and catch-up belongs on hotdogs and hamburgers. It's a hard game to play. I know; I'm a coach." There's very little structure in college, especially when you're dealing with first generation college students whose parents didn't go. This approach to time management can be geared for a work schedule as well. It doesn't matter where you are. Among other things, their schedules needed to *INCLUDE AN HOUR EVERY DAY FOR KEEPING PHYSICALLY FIT*. Everything was left up to the students. *I believe in making people responsible for their choices* and not necessarily trying to tell them what to do. In order to teach students to manage their study time effectively, I developed a concept called "study buddies." Each one had to pick someone in the class with whom to study, and they had to go over their activity schedules together and give each other feedback. Once "study buddies" had been chosen, I had them form groups of "buddy buddies" – including at least one member of the opposite sex. I thought this was important not only for socialization purposes but also in order for the students to see what the other gender's thoughts were on things. Every Monday class started with five minutes in which the groups got together and shared their activity schedules and gave each other feedback. Some of them were married or had jobs, some of them were participating in athletics, and I could see that they were headed for nervous breakdowns if their activities took up so many hours that they couldn't get enough rest.

This personal discipline of the Daily Activity Schedule is important because I think education and **most things are best done when there is a process - Process Education.**

Rules for learning

When every semester began, I introduced my students to several tools for learning, the first of which was "*The Three P's*": every day, I told students they needed to be *1) Present, 2) Punctual and 3) Prepared*. I drummed these words into them so often that after a few weeks all I had to do was hold up three fingers and they would know what I meant. Sometimes there were five "P's," meaning *Prior Preparation Prevents Poor Performance*.

There are three very important rules I tried to teach to all my students: Rule Number 1 is "*Keep your mouth closed, observe and learn*"; Rule Number 2 is "*Keep your nose out of other folks' business_unless they beg and pay you*"; and Rule Number 3 is "*Research, plan, and produce.*" I always told my students that if they could understand and follow the first one, that meant a BS degree; if they could do both 1 and 2, that meant a master's degree; and if they could follow all three rules, that would mean a Ph.D. Sometimes a student would come to me and say, "Coach, I still have not passed Rule 1. I can't keep my mouth closed. I'm not even thinking about Rule 2!"

Lifelong learning starts at an early age

My philosophy is that we should improve daily, and that it is a never ending process and that **"every day, in every way, I am getting better and better and better"** such that you develop a love for education. I think people develop that love for it if they're doing things that are exciting and that they consider as improving self. That concept has to be fostered in the schools. There are all kinds of schools of thought on education, but I think first of all there has to be a desire, and that has to come from the individual. They have to be motivated: intrinsically or extrinsically.

Educating children and teaching them the love of learning is critical. Parenting is a key way in which children learn, as is the school system. I'm going to list the major goals of the American school system, adding my own interpretation of each. The first is to achieve "mastery of basic skills, of the fundamental processes." (I call that *"reading, writing and arithmetic."*) Next is "career or vocational education" – in other words, "an individual person's satisfaction with life will be significantly related to the person's job satisfaction." (That's what I call *"a decent job."*) "Intellectual development" is the next goal. Life is complex, and I say, *"You need to know what time it is."* "Enculturation" refers to the individual's relationship with other people, the entire society, our values, etc., his or her sense of belonging. My interpretation is that *"you need to be able to get along with other people."* "Autonomy" means that you need to be competent in dealing with certain individual responsibilities and to have the ability to develop on your own. I consider that *"self-reliance."* "Citizenship" means that we need people who can be good citizens and participate in the political process. I call that *"a good, productive, participating citizen."* "Creativity and aesthetic perception" means *"appreciation for the fine arts."* "Self Concept" means that you need to be able to have your own personal goals and aspirations and to have a healthy sense of yourself, which I call *"self esteem."* "Emotional and physical well-being" I call *"a healthy individual."* "Moral and ethical character," which means that we need to be able not necessarily to determine right from wrong, because those definitions change as time goes on, but to do those things that society has found to be best for everybody at this point in time. To me that means *"decent moral values."* The twelfth goal is "self-realization," and I like to use the phrase the U.S. Army coined, *"Be all that you can be."* I want to add a thirteenth goal, which is *"spiritual awareness."* The school systems have trouble including this one because of legal rulings, but I believe this is one of the most important aspects of what we need from education.

Intergenerational Collaborative "EnTergy" (ICE")

Education in the schools will be enhanced or most effective when we educate the parents along with the students. I have a process called "Intergenerational Collaborative 'Entergy'," which addresses that need. When I say "inter-generational," I'm thinking that there should be a link of various people from conception through death. I like to look back to what I call the natural order of things. That means that before we could conceptualize it, it existed. It patterned a natural order. I can't say that God ordained it, but if we didn't know things there would be some type of order that would just take place instinctively, in a Darwinistic way.

If we go back to the first man and woman (I don't know whether they were Adam and Eve or not, but there had to be a first male and first female at some point in time), they existed as community. They got older and they had children. So then you had a group of people who were just developing, and they were within one context. For survival, some had to work, some had to have the children, and somebody was going to die. The people who started living first knew a lot more about what was going on than the others, so talking and using a language to communicate must have been only at the most rudimentary level. Language had to be developed later. They figured out what needed to be done, and they did it such that everybody in the clan or tribe could survive. The elders, for the most part, did the education of the young, because they had the time and the wisdom.

I believe we still need that type of relationship. It doesn't necessarily have to be family, but there needs to be an attachment – an interconnecting relationship – between people from the time a child is born to the time he/she dies. Somewhere in society - in the family, in the school system, or the church, or somewhere else – we need to let everyone know that people always need help and assistance and there is a network for you. Your children never actually grow up completely. They're your children forever. I don't think people often have this mindset when they get married or start a family, but I firmly believe the philosophy that "*they're my children, and as long as I'm living and they're living it is my responsibility to continue to teach them, to help them if they*

want to learn. " I have always tried to be open and available and let my children know that if they have a problem they can always bring it to Daddy. That doesn't mean I'm going to automatically solve it for them, but I'm always there to talk and give guidance and support.

Somehow or other we have to develop this philosophy in the community, and I believe it can be done best through faith organizations. I am personally very active in a number of faith groups and other community organizations. We try to get the message into the churches and the schools that everybody needs some help, and we're here to help and serve one another. Unless we can do something to educate and assist parents, they will not be equipped to educate their children in turn. I think retired people are the most valuable reservoir of knowledge we have. We need to find more and better ways to take advantage of all they have to offer our young people. We find that if we develop a relationship between the youngsters and the senior citizens — the grandparents — then we get the parents involved too. Everybody learns.

A gift from my parents

I have always had varied interests. I thank God that my mother and father were both teachers. There were always books in our home; there was always learning. There was very little radio and no television when I was a child. I played ball and studied. That was all I did. I knew my daily activity schedule (even though I didn't know that's what it was), I knew when I was going to get up in the morning, when I was going to school, when I was going to come home and do my chores, and after that, when I was going to do my homework. Then I knew I was going to go out and play. Then I was going to come inside and eat dinner, and then I was going to do some more studying. Then at 9:00 the lights were going out and I was going to go to sleep. That's just the way it was. I have a lot of respect for young people today because there are so many things out there now that were not here when I was growing up. There were no drugs that we knew of; there was booze, but nobody made it available to kids; there were gangs, but good gangs. It was just a great time.

Some things to do.

V.   **EDUCATION:**

1. Go to the local library; get a library card if you don't have one.

2. Make sure all family members do the same.

3. Plan a **family** trip to your local library.

4. Have the library take you on a library tour explaining all the services available to you.

5. Log on to a computer and brows the Internet.

6. Schedule a family library party.

7. Find a _good_ _COACH_.

8. Do what _you_ want to do!

MENTALITY

What does it mean?

The dictionary definition is "relating to the mind's capacity; how much it can absorb." In my own definition, I think mentality is one's ability to deal with abstract and practical matters such that it is in his or her best interest. It sometimes can be referred to as IQ, meaning a tangible way to test one's ability to deal with finite and abstract things. There are different lines of thought regarding whether IQ's can be improved. Some researchers say that what you're born with, what your parents bring to the table, is basically what you're going to have. I've found that people have different intelligence quotients on different things. Some people look at that as aptitude and achievement. Those are rather nebulous words, because when you start dealing with one's mental capacity, there are a lot of things that play into one's ability to comprehend, such as diet, environment, school environment, and so forth. The main thing I want people to know is that they do have a mental component that they should try to develop as much as they possibly can without thinking that there are limits, because I think **the only limits that exist in anything are in one's mind**. As long as you can let your mind flow, anything is possible. Now I'm not saying that if you have an IQ of 80, you're going to be a rocket scientist. But I am saying that you should never limit yourself or your children or anybody based on what the IQ tests (or SAT's) state. It all depends upon the individual's capacity. The message that I want to get across is that **there are no limits. Developing your mentality is an infinite process.** Now in developing the mental aspect, you also have to consider the emotional aspect. And Webster's defines emotions as "intense feelings of love, pain, fear, jealousy." As long as you're aware that those feelings exist, you'll be all right. I think that **the only two real emotions are love and fear;** all the rest are ramifications of either incomplete or distorted love or fear. I might even want to go a bit further and say that the only real emotion is love. If love is there, all those other things will cease to exist. I don't think they really exist in nature. If you look at animals, they don't really have any fear. Those are learned emotions. Many mental illnesses come from fears that we have engendered somewhere along the way; and these fears often affect our mental picture of how things need to be. I think a lot of times we put too much emphasis on one's ability to handle things from a mental standpoint, so that we frighten people.

Setting the right tone with children

The way that parents socialize their children can set them up to fail. This happens, for example, if the adult in a child's life is always telling them, "Don't do this. You can't do that," and they are bombarded with negatives. Or if they're always talked down to: "Shut up. Sit down. Be quiet." I think in the school systems, use of drugs like Ritalin and the things that they do to inhibit kids' movement creates a problem not only for their mentality but also for their physicality. I think that the mentality of the kids now is pretty sharp. It's just that I don't think we know how to tap into that mentality. We need to be more creative in increasing that mentality. Now, if the situations in the mental settings are depressing, you set people up for anxieties and neuroses, and eventually psychoses and nervous breakdowns. We're living in a highly, highly complex world now, and you've got to bring something to the table. We can start by trying to let people know that they do have capacities, and that regardless of what it's supposed to be on the paper, they can be pretty much what they want to be. And if the individual is interested and the people that are dealing with them are interested, then I think that they have what they need to at least make a reasonable and productive living in society. *You can be what you "WORK" to be*.

Mentality and morality

Within the context of mentality we find morality too. Morality comes from one's ability to distinguish between right and wrong. According to Webster, morality is "the principles of right and wrong," or "conforming to a standard of supposedly rightly conceived behaviors." You have to be really careful when you start dealing with moral issues, because what is culturally acceptable today might be considered unacceptable tomorrow and vice versa. My philosophy is that those things that are in the best interests of the larger universe usually dictate what's moral and what is not. Those things that are self-serving to an individual or a group might not be moral in the larger framework, so you have to be very careful with your moralities. Before you try to develop hard definitions of what's right and what's wrong, you have to really look at it in a very, very empathetic light. It's very difficult to deal with emotional, moral issues without using the mentality that you bring to the table, such as logical thought, scientific thought, trying to **think outside of the box**. Using this approach is going to make your life either more pleasurable or it's going to create some psychic problems for you. Emotions alone can be problematic if you don't balance them with some logical and intellectual thinking. If you feel that your emotional state is out of balance, step back, think more logically, honestly and objectively, and give yourself some time; you can get a good balance between the two: the mental and the emotional.

Empathy and sympathy come into the picture too. It's possible to go too far on the logical, thinking side, and lose the common touch.

Mentality in business

The business side of mentality depends on what your philosophy is as a person. A friend of mine is a high level executive at a company he's been with for 30 years. When he first started out he was primarily a bottom-line man. But then they restructured, downsized, and "bottom-lined" so much that it began to hurt the integrity of the company. People began to leave them. They went to competitors, and their stock is way down now. He had a lot of stock options, and of course they dropped in value. He found out that some of the people who had been loyal and receptive to the company didn't feel that way anymore. And when they had a hurricane or flood and he wanted to get his group together, some of them didn't want to work, making overtime. He said he remembered the time when the relationship between management and the workers was so good that they would have gotten together just for him. But after so much disruption and change, they felt differently. He said he was beginning to see and understand what I had been talking about for years - **(BUPDL)**.

Balancing logic and emotion

After thinking about the issue for a number of years, although it doesn't really lend itself to a formula, I think that a 50/50 approach is best: **try to weigh in evenly with logic and emotion**. But if you have to err, err on the side of the emotions, because people usually don't have the same level of logical thought. That fluctuates. But when it gets to feelings, what hurts you usually is going to hurt me too.

I try to empathize or put myself in the situation of others regularly. Sometimes I want to be Mexican, so I'll be (act) Mexican that day. I'll eat at a Mexican café. I'll go out to one of the entertainment places wearing Mexican attire. And I have a great time. Sometimes I go to country and western too. I can tap and clog and do all of that. I think if you have a global mentality, but stay aware of the local mentality, you'll be able to handle things pretty well. I find that you can't change people's mentality most of the time, but if you throw some open-ended questions out, without making any judgments, and let them think about them, most people will rise to the occasion. **People for the most part are good**. I assume everybody is good. I think there are good people who have bad ideas, or somewhere along the line they've gotten things all mixed up. I hope this book will let them look at themselves in a new light, because really what we're doing is dissecting self and seeing how we react to these things. There is a lot of linkage between the relationship area that I talked about earlier and this area, in that if something is awry about a

128

relationship it can feel like an emotional thing. *You have to step back and do some logical thinking* and that helps you have a better perspective on relationships. If you don't do that, stress is going to be created.

Mentality and stress

Stress is defined by Webster as "any force that induces bodily or mental tension," or what I call change in balance. If I'm at rest and I get up to go out the door, that creates stress. Not enough stress to create a problem, but it causes the heart rate to go up and so forth and so on. So it's always important that you understand the physical implications of what's going on. How is it affecting you? For example, if I'm in great shape I can handle a lot more stress, a lot more emotional tension, than I can if I'm not. I'm not saying physical fitness is more important than mental fitness, but the fact is *if you're dead you can't handle any of them*.

Most of the time stress is transitory, but if it lasts a period of time, it brings on sickness. I don't think we'll ever be able to eliminate drugs, because when people get very stressed, they feel they need something to help them get back down to a state of tranquility. Some people use exercise; some people do sports; some read; but drugs seem to be a way to do it immediately if not sooner. We spend sixty billion dollars in America on illegal drugs, and I don't know how much on legal drugs. Statistics show that Americans, for the most part, spend most of their drug money on prescription drugs. Drugs let people feel good and pretend to be whoever they want to be. That's a very powerful argument. They become addicted to tranquilizers, Valium, Zanex and those types of drugs. I'm not talking about junkies. Those are the ones you see on the news and you read about, but that is only the tip of the iceberg. It's the people who are making big money on stressful jobs who are able to handle their habits that you don't see. Most of the people who get picked up are the ones who are visible - the ones on the street.

In some of the courses I taught we talked about consumer health, and the fact that when you watch television there's a pill for everything that exists. If you're scratching your nose or have a little allergy, you can get a little nose spray. Eyestrain? Put some Visine in. If you have a little cramp you can rub on a little Ben Gay. There is instant relief for whatever ails you; it's a pill generation.

The mentality to stand on your own

Our mental state is usually affected by our physical and emotional state, and our emotional state is somewhat influenced by our mental state. When I was teaching, the high school curriculum prepared a youngster at the end of the ninth grade to be able to go out and fend for himself, knowing the things that he might need to be a self-sustaining person. But your emotions are always going to come into play. And whether you're able to resolve mentally what is going to be best for you versus what you want emotionally is something that is going to bother you as long as you live. It's not necessarily going to be a problem for a college student or somebody first starting out. It's something that is pervasive in all areas, because when you grow up you should know better, but we know that that's not necessarily the case. Hopefully, most people will **learn early on that you cannot live too far beyond your immediate income**. Emotionally you might want to stretch that. Self-discipline and the ability to look at something and see which is logical and which is emotional, those problems are going to always exist. I don't care how young you are or how old you get. But you have to look at how it is going to affect you down the road. What's going to happen? What are the ramifications if I get into what I call the worst-case scenario? Sit down and think of all the good things that can happen, and also think about all the bad things that can happen. Look at what is the worst thing that can happen? Although you really can't even imagine what the worst is, you have a pretty good idea. Now if that happens and you can deal with it, then you might go ahead. **If you cannot resolve the worst-case scenario, it's best for you not to do it.** Some people say you shouldn't bite off more than you can chew. *I say bite off more than you can chew and chew it – if you REALLY want to do it.* Find a way to chew it.

Mental Illness

"Normal" only means what is average, what the average person would do. There are some people – many people - who will develop some type of illness that prevents them from acting and living "normally." Sometimes it is due to disease; sometimes it is due to stress. Sometimes a mental illness will progress from anxiety to high anxiety, to inability to cope, to neurosis, to psychosis, to eventually suicide. If you have someone in the family or in the job who is under undue stress, usually the first, best person to talk with is your husband or your wife, or mother, father or somebody that you feel close to. *Often people just need somebody to talk to.* Somebody they can sit down with and not worry about being judged or having their private conversation shared with others. Just talk to them and let them know what you think the situation is. You may be right, or you might not be, but at least you can tell them what you feel. Usually things start first with feelings, and then from feelings you go to logic. Ministers are available, counseling areas are available, and so are clinics. There are a lot of places you can go for mental problems.

Generally speaking, you want to go to the minister first, then the literature, then you go to the web, and then you go to the experts. Then you go to local people who have proven that they have had good experience with handling the particular type of situation. That doesn't mean that you can go to just any minister, because some might exacerbate the problem. But usually you can ask friends who may have had similar problems. If your friends cannot help you, perhaps they can refer you to someone who can. I don't know much about psychiatry and psychotherapy. They're okay if you've got the money, but most of the time people don't have the money to seek those options. But there are health agencies within all counties where you can go and get help if you need it.

Screening for mental difficulties

There are mental tests available, and in college in the freshmen wellness classes, there is a section that deals with mental health. I would suggest that all families purchase a health book from the neighborhood bookstore. There is a self-assessment test that enables students to know if they have certain problems or tendencies and what to do to address them. _**You must be mentally sound in order to deal with the other critical aspects of your life**_, so being aware of potential problems is essential to every person, regardless of age or situation.

Some things to do.

VI.   ***MENTALITY:***

1. *Go to the library and search the Internet for materials to enhance your mental capacity.*

2. *Share with your family.*

3. *Talk to the family members about the importance of developing their mental capacity infinitely.*

4. *Find a good COACH.*

5. *Do what you want to do!*

PHYSICAL FITNESS

What is it?

The dictionary defines the physical as "development and care of the body ranging from simple calisthenics to training in health, fitness and hygiene." I believe the physical is the incarnation of the spiritual. Because I'm a physical being, I'm also a spiritual being. I think my spirituality is in the place called "heaven," that there's a Harvey Heartley already up there, and that what he is contemplating from the mind and the spirit is being acted out down here. I don't necessarily know that that's where I'm going when my body dies. The body is simply a vehicle to enable you to carry out your thoughts and your words in another realm. But be that as it may, we are physical. We are born into the world, and there are certain physical things we need in order to function and do whatever it is we want to do. *Specifically, I'm talking about rest, food, lifestyle, and*, to make sure that the physical self is maintained at the optimum level, *exercise*.

We know from Maslow's Hierarchy of Needs that we've got to have air, water, food, sex - those needs are programmed on our "hard-drives." We also need to have rest, something I don't think Americans get enough of. In college, most of the students come to class sleepy, and without having eaten breakfast. They've broken two of the cardinal rules of maintaining the physical self. They haven't gotten proper nutrition and they haven't gotten proper rest. In addition to needing good nutrition and enough rest, the body is a machine and it works better when it's exercised. With computers, cars, elevators, and video games pervasive, we often do not get the exercise that we need to keep our bodies going as they should. The fourth component that is critical to maintaining ourselves physically is avoiding excesses in the area of alcohol, sex and drugs.

Now this is not a textbook on these subjects, but I want to let you know that they do exist and you have to know what is your philosophy on your physical health per se. What do you know about it? **What is your philosophy?** What is your philosophy on rest? What is your philosophy on nutrition? What is your philosophy on exercise? Once you get to those things, you can go to the literature to find out what's what. Even if you don't think you have a philosophy, you do; it's just not defined and you're not aware of it.

I think that people should visit their libraries about once a week. I have textbooks that I've taught from for years, but numerous books are available in the library. People should do quick studies if they don't have enough time to read several books on a particular subject. Go to a bookstore, the college bookstore, or to a library, or go on line, look up fitness and whatever subject within that category you want to learn about, you can get a quick, capsulated update.

My own philosophy on physical Fitness

If you're feeling good physically, and you are able to work what I call a "normal day" (8AM - 6PM) and then have enough energy left at the end of the day to socialize or engage in some leisure time activities or recreation for two or three hours, which you need to sort of regenerate yourself, you'll be all right. Ask yourself how you feel. Are you able to carry on a normal workday, whatever your work is, with enough energy at the end of the day for recreation or activities with the family? If you can say yes to that question, you should be in pretty good physical shape.

There is a new trend in corporations to go to four 10-hour days and other "flexible hours" formats. The research is not clear as to how that's going to affect people over a period of time. There may be an increase in stress, people may find that they get lazy on their days off, or they may not be able to get enough rest working 10-hour days. It will take several years of research to really tell what the impact of this trend is. There's a lot of money spent on physical fitness. Everywhere you look there's a spa; there's a fitness center. A lot of churches have fitness groups that do walkathons and other events. There's a wealth of information out there on this subject.

Then to maintain that good health, get your medical checkups regularly.

Give your body a healthy routine

Many people feel tired all the time. If you do, how do you go about resolving it? Most of the time the problem is not enough rest. You should have a special time that you go to bed at night and a special time that you wake up because your body is a creature of habit. Some people say, "Well, I don't need but six hours of sleep; I don't need but seven." Some people need eight or nine. *Eight hours of sleep is the general rule of thumb*, and I'm talking about deep sleep. If you get eight good hours of sleep, where six of those are what we call REM sleep – Rapid Eye Movement – that's usually a good night's sleep. We've got to cut the TV off and eliminate all distractions in order to get good rest. If you shortchange yourself and don't get enough rest, stress is going to come up; allergies are going to come up; all types of things will happen to you and you may not be aware of why they are happening.

The structure of the brain and the nervous system is such that all of those things that were primitive, we still have. They're still in the back of our brains. We're the only beings that developed a big forebrain from the spine. So everything that's autonomic, like our breathing and moving our legs, is handled by the ganglia in the back of our brains and all the front brain is mainly for creative-type things. We didn't really develop a complex brain until we decided that we wanted to become human, because everything else was programmed. We did it by instinct. Those prehistoric traits are still there and, as evolution has added on to it and added on to it, the brain has developed and developed, and we have taken on what we call humanistic traits as well. In certain instances, and under certain pressures, we can revert right back to those things that the animals used to do. So everyone needs to know that there is a physical area of their life that needs to be finely tuned and you need to be intelligent about all of this. You can take it as far as you want to take it in either direction: You can look like Arnold Schwarzenegger or you might look like Teeny Weeny. You can be healthy in either instance, but there are certain basic things that everybody needs to do.

Set an example for your children

Most of our philosophies come from our parents. We are brought up in a household and we as children, usually by example, do what our parents do. We don't necessarily do what they say to do; we hear what they say, but children are always watching the grownups. So if you are living a good physical life, your children will do that too. If you have a bedtime for them and a time for them to get up and you have structure around when they eat; what they eat; if they exercise; if they get their physicals; then you will be teaching them how to live a physically sound life. If they see you staying away from an inordinate amount of alcohol, cigarettes or drugs, chances are they're going to do that too. There's an old saying that actions speak louder than words.

Problems with alcohol, tobacco and drugs can happen at an early age

- especially alcohol and tobacco. We see them advertised; we see people use them - role models - and it's made to look chic, But it's against your best interests to use those things. The Daily Activity Schedule that we had has a little section in it that asks you what your views are on this subject, and how you handle things. *It's called a health assessment.* In any good health book on the web, you can make an assessment of your health, and it'll ask you if you use these things, if you don't use them, or if you use them in moderation. That is a big part of your physical health, because you can slide into abuse very, very easily. I'm not even going to get to that here, but you need to know that there are programs out there and you need to know how you get into them. *Prevention is the best thing. When it comes to any detrimental acts, the best thing is to prevent it from happening.*

When you don't take care of yourself, it shows

I taught health for 40 years, and when you teach you observe youngsters and you find out a lot about their lifestyles. You observe their eyes. You observe if they're slouching, if they're asleep, if they have any particular nervous tics, if they're in class on time, if they seem to be hungry, what they talk about. College students usually do not get enough rest, and usually they do not get the proper food. Although there is a dining hall available, if students have 8 o'clock classes and they get up later than they should, they don't eat breakfast, and it starts to tell. They start "nabbing" (what I call eating nabs). Often they're away from home for the first time, and before they know it, it's midterm and they have tried to get acclimated and they'll come and tell me, "Coach, I've got a problem." Some of them will have drug problems. Some of them will have sexual problems. Because some of them were not brought up in an environment of informed, knowledgeable parents, they don't really know what's going on. When

145

they get on the college campus with people from everywhere, all over the country, they are apt to take the path of least resistance. They're nice students, and then all of a sudden they're in trouble.

In my classes, students had to tell me their weekly plans; they had to fill out what I called a Daily Activity Schedule, and then they had to look at **the 13 cardinal principles of education** so that when they left school they made sure that at least they knew what they were. Then I gave them a health and fitness guide. It showed them how to structure their lives based on a 10-hour day: what time you get up, etc. They had to fill those out for me every week for a month, and then after that they did it each month. The purpose was to give them a monthly checklist of what they were doing in their classes, their work, their sleep, and other elements of their lives. They had to get up in front of the class and talk to people about those things. For some of them it was the first time they'd had that kind of structure. Not only the students but adults too. When you are teaching and coaching, and you're Athletic Director as well as a family man, you have to have some structure because if you don't you've got a big blob of chaos. And people don't function well in chaos. If you know what you've got to do, when you've got to do it, chances are you'll do it. But if you don't have structure, it can get away from you in a moment's time.

I carry around a little card with me every day that tells me what I'm supposed to do that day. The a.m. is on one side and the p.m. on the other. So if I get distracted or off schedule, I can always go back to that card and get my day back in order. At the end of the day I take a look at it and compare how my day went to how I wanted it to go. Then the next day when I get up I know what I didn't get done; I know whether I'm going to feel good or whether I ran my mouth and didn't do much.

I don't let myself get away with much. My high school coach always told me, "You might fool some people. I don't recommend that you fool anybody," he said, "But ***don't ever, ever fool yourself.***" So you have to keep examining your life because a lot of times we fool ourselves and we don't know we're doing it. It's easy to do. That whole denial thing is very powerful.

Handling health problems

There are three ways that we handle any health problem: **prevention, education, treatment and rehabilitation**. We call this **"PETR."** First we try to prevent it. We try to use the vaccination or whatever. And then we educate people on it so that they are aware of what's out there. And then if those two don't take care of it, then we have to treat it. Finally, there's rehabilitation.

Your job can affect your physical self

There are some instances when people will put you in positions that you don't either have the skills or the desire to do, and once you get there, you find out that this is not really where you should be. You usually end up in that situation because there's more money or more prestige in the new position. Finding yourself in the wrong job can cause heart attacks and stress. It's not necessarily the job that causes the physical problems, it's the fact that you're not equipped to deal with the job, either from a skill standpoint or in terms of passion for the work. Some people thrive in high stress jobs and some don't. My wife used to say, "You go all the time! It's basketball, basketball . . . .You're going all the time! Slow down, relax, live like normal people." It was a problem for her, but not for me. I enjoyed that. My son said I just liked the action. I do.

Some things to do.

VII.   **PHYSICAL FITNESS:**

1. Look at the Do-It-Yourself
    fitness guide in the Quick-Look
    section.

2. Visit the local library and the
    World Wide Web articles, books,
    tapes, and videos on fitness
    programs.

3. Check your daily activities
    schedule and find time for
    workouts.

4. Design your own fitness program.

5. Find a _good_ COACH.

6. Do what _you_ want to do!

YOUR FINANCES

Define it first

According to Webster, finance is "the management of money affairs, based on the resources that are available." I think that finance is the ability to have resources available as a result of managing your affairs in a timely fashion, but also **always to have more than you need.** That's **financial health: to have it whether you need it or not.** That's my philosophy.

Linkages between finance and lifestyle

How you manage the money or resources that are available to you as a person is going to determine whether you have a nice, pleasant life, or whether you're going to be running from the collectors. My philosophy on finance is that you should choose work doing something that you like, and find someone willing to pay you enough money to live the lifestyle you think you should have. Usually, the problem in the financial arena is not that we don't have enough money. It's that the things that we want far outstrip our ability to buy them. And that is mainly because of television and other ways that we are exposed to how other people live who make a lot more money than we do (The Joneses). We want those lifestyles, and there's nothing wrong with aspiring to any type of lifestyle. But **the amount of money that you have should dictate your lifestyle.** There are various lifestyles that you can have based on the amount of money that you have. It's like in athletics: you can be participatory, you can be competitive, or you can be championship. But all of them come with different payrolls.

Personal Financial Planning

As soon as you become employed, or you have resources coming in – you might already have some that has been left to you, for example, – **you should have a financial plan.** You should know where your money's going to be coming from - weekly, monthly, or however you're being paid. Once that money is coming in, you should track it for about six months to see how much is coming in and how much is going out.

You have to have **a financial plan** - most people call it a **budget.** I don't like to use the word budget because it frightens people. They think of a lot of numbers and sophisticated formulas and calculations. But I recommend that you use a very simplistic way of tracking your finances. I always start at the beginning of the month, because the calendar is always organized. You always know when September or October is coming. So if you can start at the beginning of the month it will give you a pretty good idea of the funds that come in during the month.

It's very simple to get a sheet of paper and put down the beginning of the month: October 1st. You have little columns, and you get a little book, composition book, costs you 98 cents, and you have **what you owe, what you paid, what your balances are**, and the check number or money order that you paid it with. In the left column after you've done that you put **Income**, that's ***Roman numeral I. Roman numeral II is Savings.*** And just as the Bible says tithing is giving 10%, it's arbitrary, but it makes the mathematics easy because all you have to do is move a decimal point. So you want to ***pay yourself first***, because if you wait until the end to pay yourself, there's never going to be any money. Uncle Sam takes out his income tax, the state takes out its income tax, and all those intangibles first, and you never miss it because you never see it. So what you're going to do is ***tax yourself, just like Uncle Sam: State, federal, me*** (see financial chart). Take 10% of that and put it up in Savings. That's Roman numeral II. Then the next thing you're going to have is ***Necessities, Roman numeral III.*** Now Necessities are what you cannot live without. A lot of people mix up wants and necessities, because they want some things very, very badly. They put them in the Necessity category, but they are not necessities. A necessity is what you have to have to live, to function: ***food, clothing and shelter***, for example. In a society such as the one

154

we have there are a lot of other things that at one time were not necessities but they are now, such as the **gas bill, electricity, car insurance, telephone,** etc. Those are things that you really have to have in order to function. They go next. Then after that, you have what I call **Installments. Installments should never run more than 10% of what you bring home** either, to be safe. That gives you a little balance to buy "big ticket" items over a period of time. Then after that you get **Personals** and other little things that usually run about 5%.

Because you're starting out, your Necessities are going to take up about 65% of your income. In some instances they will take more; in some instances less. These are just ballpark figures. But for a few months it gives you a chance to see where your money is going. And it gives you a systematic check on whether you're spending more money on some things than you should. It keeps you from being in denial – unconscious denial.

Another concept that we need to understand is **"bring home" pay.** What you make and what you bring home are different. What you earn is gross, but all you can actually function with is what you're going to bring home. You have to find ways to minimize your taxes but legally pay your fair share. And you'll find that *as you make more money, it takes more money.* The best way to learn these concepts is to go to the literature that's available or go on line and do research. And you can buy software to do just about anything you want to do.

Credit cards and credit lines are not recommended when you're just starting out except for items that are necessary - not for ball games and other discretionary things - because *credit cards are one of the biggest traps that young people can fall into.* (People who are not so young fall into the credit card trap as well!) These numbers can be tweaked, depending upon your particular situation. At the end of the page *you'll have totals: total owed, total paid, and total balance.*

I'm assuming that you're going to keep your job, or whatever your income is, for a reasonable amount of time. And if you lose that job you can get another one because you've

been educationally sound, and you've
been professionally sound. So you can
readily assume that you're going to
always have a pretty good salary for
at least a year. At the end of the
fiscal year you might get a raise or
you might get cut, but you know what
you've done for that year. *Owning
your own business is best, if you so
desire.*

Not everyone will start in
January. The corporate fiscal year is
usually from July 1 to June 30th,
particularly for governments,
businesses and colleges. Regardless
of what period you start with, I
suggest that in January you look at
what happened the year before. Look
at your book and you'll get a pretty
good idea of your financial
lifestyle. You might find that you
want to up it, or you might find that
you have wasted funds that you should
have done better with. But when you
start in January of that year you
should have some kind of idea or plan
of what you're going to make, what
you want to save, what you want to
do, where you're going to go. At some
point you should *start trying to save
money for investing.* Usually you
don't want to invest until you have

at least six months of money saved, so that if something happens you can live for six months without going up in smoke. Once you have that set aside, you can refer to any number of good financial books to get you started in investing. You can go to the web and find out a lot of things too. All of the major brokerage houses have web sites and publications to guide you. You can also get software that will show you how to do your financial planning and how to manage your investments. But most of the time people don't want to follow the plan. *They want to have what they want to have. IMMEDIATELY.*

Once you are working, you want to make sure that when you reach retirement age you can live reasonably well for the rest of your life. It's important that you don't have "too much age at the end of the money." With the likelihood of Social Security shortfalls in the future, it is the individual's responsibility to take care of him or herself. And *the secret is to start at an early age,* usually shortly after you start working.

Financial advice for young people

I was fortunate to have started out teaching mathematics in high school in the mid-50's. Back then I taught a course called General Math, which was excellent because it dealt with all of the things that a student who was going to drop out of high school at the ninth grade needed to know. (Back in the 50's a lot of students didn't want to go past age 15 or 16 in school.) So all of the basic practical financial things that they needed to know were in that course. Young people who were planning to go to college were jumping to take algebra, trigonometry, calculus and geometry, but I thought they should have had that basic course too, because it dealt with the American consumer. As I look back over the students I taught in high school, I find that a lot of them who didn't go to college are as financially sound as some of the ones I taught the higher math. Some of them are having problems, or they had problems, because they never really understood the American economy and the things that they should have done. The students who took the basic course were not considered very "academically skilled", but it was a great course and they really learned something practical. I learned some things when I taught it. By having taught it, I put it into practice, and I found that the basic lesson of the course was that *if you're going to live from month to month, you've got to be able to handle your finances. You're going to get old, so you might as well start investing at an early age.* If you start early it's like a snowball going down the hill; it just gets larger and larger. After a while you can't stop it. I have tried to teach that to my youngsters and my children, and they're pretty satisfied. They have portfolios of their own.

Many young people have an interest in being financially sound because they had grandparents living in their homes while they were growing up. A lot of them see that when their parents reach that age they are going to be in some pretty serious situations. Youngsters have a keen sense of being able to project if you let them. If you can relate the material to where they are and what they're dealing with; if you ask them, "Well, now, what are the things you see that are going to happen to you when you get to be sixty?" they'll often say, "Well, you know, Grandma and they are living with us. We have to take care of them." If you don't start at an early age putting some money aside for *you*, then you're going to be in that situation also.

I was introduced to financial concepts early

I was eleven when I started saving my money. I had very good parents, and my mother and I had to fend for ourselves at an early age. My father was in the Navy for four years during World War II, and we didn't have extra funds to do a lot of things; this made me more financially responsible. When my father came home from the Navy we had to live frugally because he was going to college on the GI Bill.

We had to manage our money very carefully, but it taught us a lot of things, and the things that they learned, I learned too. I was sort of like a brother, sister and a son to them because of my age and the fact that I was helping out so much. I was right there in the midst of it, and it truly helped me. My grandparents owned a corner store, farms and rental property. They always included me in the businesses because I was the oldest, and for a long time the *only*, grandson. My grandparents were getting old, so I helped out. I had a pretty good business mentality by the time I was in my early teens. I knew how to run a farm - we did tobacco, cotton, truck farming, the whole nine yards. I was not "directly involved" because I was the grandson, but I was around; I listened; I saw what went on. I helped to stock the grocery store shelves. I learned about credit very early.

I would come home in the afternoons and they would take a nap, and I would run the store. I would put the stock up. I would mark the prices. I would check everything out. I would put the bills up there.

My grandfather had a lot of those little composition books where he had given people credit. My granddaddy said to me, "Now you see those books up there?" I said, "Sure." He said, "Well those books are full of people owing me money. And I don't do any more credit business." He said, "Now they're going to see that you're in here and they're going to come down and want to get credit, and they'll think you don't know. They'll have all kinds of stories for you. Some of them will be true. But we don't do any credit business because all you see in those books is money that is owed to me by some people in the neighborhood. And if you look on the shelf, we pay cash for all of that stuff when it comes in. Now if we don't sell something, we can eat it or use it up. It's ours. But if you give it away to people who say they're going to pay you, you're going to end up with some more books. Now sometimes I make personal decisions to let people have things. I don't look for it back. I might put it in the book. Sometimes if I think I might want to do that, I do that. But you can't. You can't make those decisions."

He continued, "The second thing is everything that goes in the cash register does not belong to us. You'll see that there will be a lot of money in there, but you've got to realize that bills and taxes and things have to be paid for, so don't think we're getting rich by looking in the cash register. You've got to keep the books and then you'll continue to find out where the money goes."

My granddaddy was also my Sunday School teaching superintendent and that was back at a time when I was the only grandson. Now, years later, I'm finding out there's a certain biological attachment between grandparents and grandchildren. He would always say, "Where you want to go, boy?" I was like another son to him. I would ride in the truck with him, and I just had a marvelous childhood. I learned a lot, and the grownups didn't try to pull the wool over my eyes. Whatever I wanted to talk about, that's what we talked about. I was never intimidated. There were never any subjects that were off limits. Whatever I wanted to know about, we sat down and talked about it.

I'm realizing more and more how nice it was to have someone like that in my life. I didn't realize that back then, but I've always been sort of a free spirit, and I've always been able to *get past the thought*

police; I've always been able to **think outside of the box.** And those attributes have helped me from a financial standpoint.

Wants versus needs: understanding what's important

My family was black middle class. We always lived comfortably. In the late 40's and early 50's, after World War II, it was almost before television in small towns and many people in small towns didn't have cars. The country was beginning to rebuild. My family had a car; we had a phone; we had a house. My parents had jobs teaching school. We had income, and I never was hungry. I never had any kind of bad experiences. We were by no means wealthy, but I never felt deprived.

I learned how to make decisions about what were necessities versus what were wants - what was important. I knew there was going to be a paycheck every month. I knew that the bills were going to be paid and that there was going to be food on the table. I knew I was going to have clothes and that I would be warm.

Basically, that's all I really needed. I had a basketball, a football and a baseball, and I didn't need all the other stuff.

I worked on the farms, and in the summers I went to Connecticut and lived with some of my cousins. I got to know the North and I got to know the South. My cousin would come down and spend some time with me and we'd work in tobacco and cotton, and we'd buy our clothes with the money we made.

I didn't experience racism personally. I knew that it existed, but I lived in a black community and I knew where the white community was. The black and white kids would get together and play (until the white kids' parents would break us up). But I didn't have "white friends." You just didn't go to their houses, but we played ball together secretly. When the parents didn't interfere we had a great time. I had a good childhood. We knew what was going down, but it was just something that you didn't necessarily talk about at that time. There were things that we didn't think were right, but we were not adults, so we didn't get into that.

Consider various time horizons when you plan

When you develop your financial plan you need to set your **immediate objectives**, which cover now or the next week or so, and then you have **short term objectives**, which might cover a year or two, and then you have your **long term objectives**, which might be from five to ten years. Then you have what I call **very long term objectives**, which is past that. And finally I have added another category that I call **financial objectives for eternity**.

What are your financial plans for after you die? Seniors today have a tremendous amount of strength politically, because there are so many of them, and they've lived so long. They're more intelligent because they've lived longer. And naturally they want things to benefit them. I see in the future a sort of age war in which the seniors will want more and more things at the expense of the younger people who have to pay for those things. There are going to be more seniors and fewer young people, and mathematically it's just not going to work.

This has opened up a debate as to what to do with the Social Security money. I'm not an economic expert, but I think young people should put some money aside for their retirement and not rely on Social Security and Medicare alone to take care of them in their old age. There are two ways they can do this: they can put it aside from their jobs, because there are people who are in better shape to handle it and to invest it than they are; then some of the money that I said they were putting in savings, they should start trying to do something else with on the side, such as an IRA. I think they should put away at least 10% of their earnings. Even the squirrels do that. ***That's your 10% savings. Pay yourself first.***

A.G. Gaston was an Atlanta businessman who died a few years ago. He was written up in one of the first issues of Ebony in the late 50's, and I cut that article out and put it on my wall. He was a role model for me. One of the things he said in that article was, **"*Pay yourself first.*" I *never forgot that.***

Think about retirement early

It's every individual's responsibility to take care of him or herself. I don't think that the natural order of things would have it such that somebody else is supposed to take care of you. You should do that yourself. You've got the tools to do it. I hope the parents and teachers and other people who read this book will know that it is everybody's responsibility to start, at as early an age as possible, thinking about the time when they will not be able to work physically.

Now if you're doing something you enjoy, you don't necessarily need to retire. Working keeps you young. It keeps the blood moving and the brain working. Many people don't feel good and they get diseases because they're not doing anything; they're bored; they're depressed and they don't know it. And that's because they're not doing things that they enjoy doing. Even if you stop working, you should have a hobby that you enjoy. The best situation is to **find a hobby that you love, and find a way to get paid for doing it.** Because once you are making enough money to live the way that you want to live, you'll be all right.

More is never enough.

People think they need more, more, more. Well, you have to learn how to master yourself. Find out what is important and what is not, and then just go with the flow. And don't even get on these stress tracks, because even if you're making an enormous amount of money, chances are you're under an enormous amount of stress. I've found out they're directly proportional to each other. You're not going to make a lot of money unless you have a lot of responsibility. If you love it, fine; if you don't, then you're aching for a stress attack.

This is an easy trap to fall into, because people go to college, they go to job training and they get on the track and then they want to have big beautiful homes, big beautiful cars, all of those things. There's nothing wrong with that kind of lifestyle, as long as you're willing to pay the price that it's going to ream from you. Usually when you're young you have that energy. As you get older you may not feel like you want to do that as much. I'm not saying you shouldn't have these things. They're great. But **do not to be a slave to your possessions.**

Enlightenment means that you can live without any of the physical things that most people consider so important. There is a magazine called "Enlightenment" in which gurus, people who have supposedly found nirvana, are interviewed about their philosophies of life. I would suggest that anyone who really wants to find out about themselves and about the natural order of things and spirituality should read that magazine. It makes you internalize and think within yourself, and that's really where everything comes from. **Nobody really has the answer.** Anybody's answer is as good as anybody else's, if you actually believe it.

When you're in financial trouble

For people whose financial life needs some improvement, the first thing to do is look at your financial notebook or your financial plan book. Study it carefully – the money coming in and the bills you've accumulated – in order to *clearly understand your specific financial situation*. The next step is to *get some help*. In larger cities there is a program called *"Family Consumer Services,"* and that is a *Health and Human Services program* that is funded by the federal, state and local governments.

You can go to them with all your bills, and all of your receipts and tell them, "I'm in bad shape." (This is not the same as filing for bankruptcy, or Chapter 11.) You can go to them any time. They will look at what you have, appoint you a counselor, look at your books, and tell you what you need to do. The first thing they do is ask you for your credit cards. They say, "In order for us to help you, you've got to *give up your credit cards*." They have a big jar full of cut up credit cards. Then they figure out how much money you bring in and how much you need to live on based on your bills.

They come up with a plan for you. If you agree to that plan, they will call all your creditors; they will restructure your monthly payments to fit within your monthly income, and they will pay your bills for you. But you have to give them a certified check when you get paid. It can't be late.

When people approach me because they have gotten into a financial hole, I send them there to get straightened out. As long as you have a job and you can make the payments, they will help you get out, but it takes a lot of discipline because you've developed some bad habits and dug a hole for yourself. They will counsel you concerning some of the things that you might have wanted in the past that you can't really afford to have. You go in once a month for counseling to see how you're doing. You keep your same records - your financial book. *But most of the time people don't write things down, so they don't know - especially things that they don't want to know. I call this selective denial.*

Budgeting itself is not that hard, but the idea may seem intimidating.

I suggest that you use a cardboard box to keep your bills in. Some people pay bills weekly, some pay them at the first of the month. Usually if you make enough money you just pay them once a month because most of them come at the first of the month. So since it comes at the first of the month it's best to just list it, and you put it down, and you know where you are. It won't get lost because you know where it is. If you do the math, it's very simple. I've found that it's not that people don't know, it's that they just really don't want to follow the math. Math has what we call a closure law, and that means *five plus two is always going to be seven. It's not going to be eight. Like it or not.*

Finance Course 101

1. You must have an income to match your lifestyle.
2. How much money you make largely determines your lifestyle.
3. Usually, you need a profession or trade to ensure that you have a marketable skill.
4. Pay yourself first. That's what Uncle Sam does to your check.
5. Save a minimum of 10% of your bring home pay FIRST!
6. Live below your financial means.
7. Pay cash; it's cheaper.
8. Avoid the credit card trap.
9. Keep some cash in your pocket at all times.
10. Don't try to be a fashion plate or clotheshorse.
11. You don't have to have the most expensive house or car.
12. Start slowly, study, learn, and find a PROVEN, SUCCESSFUL, FINANCIAL COACH.

Some things to do.

VIII.   <u>YOUR FINANCES</u>

1. Make out your own financial plan in your spiral notebook (See sample financial plan in the Quick-Look section).

2. Follow your plan for at least six months, adjusting as you go.

3. Share your plan with your spouse or significant other. Include your children.

4. Go to the library. Talk with the librarians. Get on-line. Do research.

5. Find a <u>good</u> <u>COACH</u>.

6. Do what <u>you</u> want to do!

PROFESSIONAL MATTERS

What's the definition?

Webster defines profession as "a calling requiring specialized knowledge and often long academic preparation." I think people sometimes get jobs and professions confused. They don't have a clear definition of a profession or a job. I think a job is anything that you do to receive some type of monetary reward. It does not necessarily require that you have the training or the skills or even the interest to do it for a long period of time. It's a paycheck. I think in this day and age, each person should be engaged in some type of profession, and I don't necessarily mean that you have to have long academic hours, or work yourself to death. **Whatever you decide to do, there should be a legal and moral need for it**, because there are some professions you can go into that are not in the best interests of society. We're talking about ones that there's a need for in society. You should prepare yourself for that at a very early age. That's where education comes in.

To choose a profession, you should find out what you really like doing best with a passion, and then get someone to pay you for doing it. Or, if you can't get someone to pay you for it, **find out how you can pay yourself for doing it**. I can't make that point too strongly, because I've seen youngsters come to college, spend four years there, and not really know what they want to do.

Preparing young people for careers

When my students were working on their Daily Activities Schedules, they also had to write out what they planned to do - what they thought they wanted to do for the rest of their lives. I taught from freshmen to seniors, but I taught a lot of freshmen because *I taught freshman wellness courses*. They were large, service classes that every freshman had to take. I didn't teach them all, but I had about two or three classes, and I would have anywhere from thirty to fifty per class. Most of them had no idea what they wanted to do. It didn't really matter to me what they wanted to do, but they had to write down their career goals. Then they had to read them to the class, and we had a two-minute question and answer period when the other students could ask why they wanted to do this.

We already had information on their backgrounds because they had had to write an autobiography for class too, so we had a pretty good feel about who they were, where they came from, etc. The career discussion was trying to tell them where they were trying to go. Their Daily Activities Schedule was trying to tell them how to get there. Once they did that, we had a Student Career Center where students would go and access a big career data bank. They would type in what they wanted to do, what their major was, and it would print out for them what the career matches were. It was like a dictionary of occupational titles, and it would not only match up what they said they wanted to do, but it would also tell them what they should have in terms of education and preparation when they got ready to get the job.

When I teach my students about getting a job, I **start from the job and go backwards**. Most people want to go to school and then get a job. I suggest analyzing the job first and then come back to see what courses you're going to need to take to the job. I ask them, once you apply for that job, what are the skills you're going to need? So they get the address and phone numbers, and they actually have to write that company a letter, tell them what their classification is, and that they want to come work with that firm. I also encouraged summer employment where they were going, including co-op programs if they had them, because most of the students needed summer employment. In those programs you work a semester, and then you're off a semester. You're employed, you're in college, and you're learning a job. I take those letters up, and they get a grade for doing that. I say they have to send letters to three companies, no more than three. Then they find out what courses they need to take, what they need to have, and what the job entails and they get an idea also of what it's like going through the process of getting a job before they get to be a senior. Most people think about what they're going to do at the end of four years. "I spent four years and I don't really want to do this". So, by having that experience early, they had a chance to find out what it was like. I told them, "Now think about what you would like to do for the rest of your life, and then figure out how you can get paid for it." Most of them think about Hollywood, the NBA, NFL, hip-hop artists, about being on talk shows, being star athletes or movie stars. I say, well now there are a lot of things you can do based on your majors and what you want to do. *You don't want to have to wake up every morning dreading to go to work* - which so many Americans do. But they were not taken through the process.

Applying the same concepts to youngsters

Likewise, when we go out and work with the youngsters in the community, we're doing the same thing with them that I was doing with college students. It focuses them. It makes them think, **"Well I've got to do something for the rest of my life."** I say, "Well you guys want to drive these big pretty cars, and have the ladies looking at you, and wear your gold. Well where are you going to get it? Selling crack is not an option because that's a pretty hazardous job. First of all you're either going to end up dead, a junkie, somebody's going to rob you, or you're going to get 20-50 years in jail. So you can't do that for a lifetime. Don't even go there. So think about what kind of lifestyle you want to have; then think about how you're going to support it; then find out what you like to do to accomplish it." I tell them **the process starts now. It starts today,** and each day you build on it, and build, and build. Then I put the letter "K" up on the board, which stands for **"kaizen."** *Kaizen* is a Japanese word that means **to continually get better**. I've found that no matter what country or what culture you're in, there is always a word that means "continually getting better and better and better." The Japanese always have that word around – *kaizen* – and I adopted it. There's another "k" word called **"kenosis,"**

which means that you "get rid of it."
You houseclean. If things in your
mind are not working, you've got to
get rid of them. You've got to throw
them away because, although they
might have been good at one time,
they serve no purpose now. Your brain
is not necessarily like a data bank,
with a limited amount of memory. It
probably has infinite information
storage capacity, but if you've got
some clutter up in there, you just
get rid of that.

"ICE" as it applies to the workplace

The educational process that I
have called "**Intergenerational
Collaborative EnTergy**" can apply to
the workplace as well. I believe that
when you come on board in a
corporation, there should be some
connection from you all the way up
through the president, or the CEO,
and that you should understand what
they do. In most organizations, you
don't know all the people who hire
you. You're brought in to fix these
little widgets, but how does the
business process in this company
work? Good companies should promote

from within, in my opinion. So although someone starts at a lower level, you don't know what his ultimate potential is. So you should let him know you have faith in him, teach him the ropes, and give him the opportunity to advance. His immediate boss has that primary responsibility, but there should also be someone above him or her, and so on up the line. So it's like a chain. Every organization should want its employees to aspire to go on to the next level, and they should encourage it. If they develop this Intergenerational Collaborative Energy in the workplace, then when the new employee comes in, he will know what's what. He will know that he may not make it all the way to the top, but he understands how the process works and it's available to everyone.

I don't encourage gossiping from level to level in a job setting to impress because when you do that it can cause jealousy and envy among coworkers. Even if the rationale for that kind of behavior is explained, people feel threatened when it comes to their jobs and their livelihood. It's the responsibility of management

to let all the workers know that they
want everybody to do well, and they
don't want anyone to feel threatened,
but that the shareholders and the
people who have invested money in the
company want the best possible
employees they can have. If you look
at it as lifelong processing, and
lifelong education, you'll continue
to grow and they'll reward you
accordingly.

Play to win

I guess that approach to work
comes from my being a coach. The only
thing I know is we've got to start
five people, and I'm going to start
the best five that I can get. Then
I'm going to come back with the next
best five. I've always had statistics
and videotape to look at, and I
always made evaluations every night.
There are stories in the newspaper
and on the radio and TV every day.
**One thing about athletics: you get a
report card immediately**. That doesn't
mean that I'm going to beg you to do
this or that. I'm just going to let

you know what the statistics are, and based on what they are, that's who's going to play. *We all want to win. It's not about you and it's not about me. It's about the team.* So let's go out and work hard, give our best. If we win, fine. If we don't, then we need to go back to the drawing board, because we're playing a win/lose game. Some people will tell you, "Well it ain't whether you win or lose." I say, "If you show me somebody who doesn't care whether you win or lose, I'll show you a loser." T-E-A-M: "Together Everyone Achieves More."

Commitment to community service starts early

When I taught school, I had class projects, and all of my classes had to do a minimum of ten hours of community work per semester. Right near the campus we had the Boys' and Girls' Club, and we had two recreation centers that were within walking distance. I was on the board for most of those Boys and Girls Clubs for nearly twenty years, and I always worked with them in assigning students to work with the girls and the boys. We devised some projects that could be done on spring and fall break. Sometimes the students had free hours, and they had to go over to the clubs and do some work. We came up with a program that had the youngsters working with the seniors. The kids in the Boys' and Girls' Club were youngsters. The recreation centers were where the older people went, and also parents.

We also have a program at St. Augustine's College called **Community Development Resources** in which the college works with the community in housing and physical fitness and the whole nine yards. We have computers there and we structure after-school programs for neighborhood kids and senior citizens who want to come and learn on the computer. Most of our athletics majors know how to do this because they have to take classes in computer sciences, so we get these students, many of whom are world-class athletes, and the kids just gravitate to them. For example, when I introduce the kids to Antonio Pettigrew, who's an Olympic gold medalist, they're enthralled! The athletes talk to the youngsters about athletics, and then they help them with their homework on the computers. The kids are so glad to be there with them.

Athletes as role models

You can do a lot of things with athletes that you can't do with other kids. When you expose youngsters to athletes they look up to, you get their attention. You start with sports and from sports you explain how they have to get to high school first. So now you've gotten them motivated. Then you teach them some techniques on how they should run, play the game, skills, etc., how they should go to bed early, how they should eat, and how they should stay out of trouble. They listen to you because they're looking up to you. Then they'll tell their parents about it. You say, "Well, tell your parents to come on down with you the next time." ***I don't care where you go, most grandparents and parents are interested in their kids***, and if you get the kids involved, you'll bring the adults into it. You say, "Well you come on down too. We need you in this process too" because you want them to be involved. So then they learn too. A lot of people are just afraid to come to the place. The building just intimidates them. But you get them there and you have punch and cookies, pizza, etc. and then you just sit down and talk. We try to get a high school athlete who's in the community to come there too. Then you're building this network, "ICE," and pretty soon you have a chain. Sometimes you'll have an overnight campout or a little picnic, or you'll go somewhere and play games. We may go down and have volleyball tournaments, softball games, track meets, and basketball tournaments on the campus. Then we see who can run the fastest so we can find out who has natural talent. Everybody has a chance to participate.

I knew my passion early in life

I was in a great profession, and I tried to be good at it all the way along. I got my first ball when I was three years old. The 7th and 8th grade boys and girls were having a tournament at school. At that time we had what we called activity periods, and I was watching the game. There was a time out, and the ball was on the free throw line, so I just ran out there on the floor and got it and went down to the goal. It was the first time I'd ever had a ball in my hands, and I tried to shoot it. So it caught on, and they threw me the ball and I tried to shoot it. I never did get it up that high, but when I came back I was smiling, and my mom said I had a great time. Well, I played ball day and night; I had a little goal in my yard. I lived not too far from the schoolyard. I could run there. I had my ball, and it just gave me great joy and pleasure. And I played day, and I played night. ***I just loved to play.***

Of course at that time, in the late 1930's and early 1940's, there was nothing else to do: there were no recreational centers; there were few TV's. At that time there wasn't even any black music that you could hear on radio. You could buy it, but they didn't play it on the radio. So we played ball. We also had a little group of boys that used to go in the woods where we had a little camp. We'd sneak our mamas' potatoes and meat - not enough that they would know some was missing. We built a log bridge, and we'd go swimming in the river. I mean we had a great time as kids. We fished. We stayed gone most of the day. Our neighborhoods were safe.

People didn't worry about where you were. They knew you were somewhere in the neighborhood and that if you did something wrong somebody was going to whip you and send you home and tell your mama, and that then you'd get another whipping. It was just a great time. Whoever got to the schoolyard first brought their ball and you just started playing. Some kids had balls, some kids didn't. There was one guy who was an only child and he had everything he wanted. He was a spoiled brat. He'd bring his ball out there, and he wanted to play every game. When you lost you were supposed to sit down, but you had to choose the next team too, and if he didn't get chosen, he'd say, "Give me my ball." Without him there was no game. Once he was playing, all the calls went his way. We had to acquiesce because he had the ball. So I got a ball and I used to just play and work on my moves and my games. I just loved it. I loved school then.

Sometimes you change your mind

I graduated from high school when I was fifteen. I was two years younger than most of the members of my class. I didn't think that it would be in my best interests to skip any grades because I wanted to continue playing, and I knew if I went up I was going to be competing against people who were more mature physically than I was. I was fourteen when I got my college scholarship. We were playing Hillside in Durham in the tournament and I threw up thirty-nine points, full court, 94/40. At that time **we played the game the way the game was supposed to be played, which was "94/40, smoke & smother."** I could run all night. I just didn't get tired. I could shut you down and keep running. If I got a shot it never dawned on me that it might not go in. I just didn't miss. I got good grades, too, and I took a college prep curriculum. So I went to college and the medical doctor in town, who was a good friend of my parents, wanted me to be a doctor. They knew that they were going to need some doctors, and I didn't have any problem with that. My freshman year I was majoring in pre-med, and I was playing ball at North Carolina Central. But I found out when I got to college that there were kids from everywhere, and the academics and the athletics was a lot tougher than it was in high school. I had to make a choice. If I was going to go to medical school, I was going to have to give up athletics. I really fell in love with athletics, so I majored in Physical Education and I had a minor in Biology. That way when I got out, if I decided I wanted to be a doctor, I could take a couple of courses and get into medical school.

I had a pretty heavy course load – trigonometry, calculus, and physics – and I was out there running too. I played under John McLendon, who I think was one of the greatest basketball minds in the world. We ran, ran, ran, ran, ran, and when we went home at night we didn't even think about going out. There was only one place we could go, and that was to bed. I was young then. I was sixteen and I was running against guys who were twenty-five and thirty – many of them World War II veterans; grown men who had families. Ultimately that got to be a bit much. They could do it, but I was still growing.

Coach was very wise. He put the freshmen together, and put them on a different floor from the older guys. During that time in athletics, and given Coach McLendon's values, the kids just didn't mess around. They didn't do drugs; they didn't drink; they didn't smoke. They kept your butt in line. It was a different breed of guy. They were just clean-cut people, not only physically but morally too, so none of that stuff went on because if they even caught anybody who thought that they wanted to get out of line, they'd whip their butts themselves. So they were like big brothers. Well all of that stuff just didn't exist. It was a different day.

When doors began to open

When I graduated in '55, there were only two black pro basketball players. A few years later, my college teammate Sam Jones played with the Celtics - with Bill Russell and all those great championship teams. The first black athlete who went to the NBA from the CIAA was a player who played at North Carolina Central University - Harold Hunter. Earl Lloyd from West Virginia State was in there too. There were some great players in the CIAA who later became NBA stars: Charles Oakley, Earl "the Pearl" Monroe, Sam Jones, Bobby Dandridge, etc.

Your career should be your passion

You should really love what you're doing; and you should want to do it if you could even without the money. But realistically, you've got to have food. You've got to support your family. We need to ask kids early on, **"What do you enjoy doing?"** We need to get them thinking about that, and then when it's time to choose a profession or a career, they will have given it some thought. That doesn't mean every kid has to get a college education. He might want to be a computer repairperson. He might want to work with CP&L. But regardless of what it is, he should bring a passion to the table.

I found something I was passionate about and found that they would pay me to do it. I would've coached for free. People talk about jobs, but I figure I've had fun all my life. It was work, but it was work that I enjoyed doing. The hours that a coach puts in are long, intense, and rough, and I think that anybody should approach his profession or his job that way. My whole life has been consumed with my family, teaching and athletics, I guess mainly because I came from a family that taught. I helped Mom and Dad correct papers when I was young. I enjoyed teaching and coaching. Then I became an Athletic Director because after I started working I found out that, although I needed a lot of things for basketball, if the football coach was AD, the football team would have spent most of the money by the time my turn came around. So at my second job I made sure that wherever I went I was also Athletic Director. I tried to be fair to all the sports because I had been in the other position. I tried to have enough resources for everybody.

"BUPDL" leadership

We had coaches' meetings, and I'd always be in what I call **"*bottoms up participatory democratic leadership*"** mode. I would always give the coaches a little checklist as to what their main problems were. They were supposed to find out those problems from the players and themselves. Then not only were they to put the problem down succinctly, but then each coach was supposed to develop his or her own solution to it along with where the money to do it was coming from.

At Athletic Directors' meetings, we'd start the year off discussing the main problems. Sometimes we would have the athletes, but the money wasn't there. We'd list the top five problems in order of importance. **(Hierarchy).** Then we would list whether we saw some possible solutions. Then we would ask, "Can we handle the problem? What do we think is required to handle it? If we can't do it ourselves, what do we think the administration should do?" Then we would estimate the cost and then talk about how we were going to raise the money. When you asked them how to raise the money, that eliminated a lot of things, so it got to that stage of the process where you pretty much knew that they actually needed it. Then once they did that, a lot of times, you could get fundraising ideas from other coaches.

Then I would go to the corporate community for certain things and get funds too. There were alumni whom I could call and say, "Well, you know we need this," or there were foundations. That gave me a way of letting them know, and usually I didn't go past the first two for all of them. Then I would get that together and present it to the administration, and then I had a rationale for it - and I would explain that this came from the players, or the coaches, as the case may be. The things that I could resolve with the coaches I did. The things that I couldn't resolve with them, I took to the administration and asked for their help. Often they would agree to handle it.

Know when it's time to leave

A coach's life is not eight to five. A coach's life is total commitment: 24-7-365. Once I reached the point that I didn't feel like total commitment, I just resigned. I knew it was time; you can feel it coming. The game is a great game. It's been too good to me for me to do less than my best. I could never do that. I wasn't raised that way. I said I've enjoyed it, but I don't honestly think I can commit the hours, the time, and the energy that are needed to keep it at the level where I have brought it any longer. My body's telling me I need to slow down. I can't work those eighteen- and twenty-hour days, day in and day out.

I resigned at a tournament game. Fourteen thousand people were there. I hadn't told anybody, except my wife, in advance. When I was sitting on that bench, I knew I didn't want to sit there anymore. At the end of the game I got the mike, and I said I'd like to make an announcement.

We had gotten barbecued. It had happened because I was getting ready to build another championship team. The school had run into some financial problems and they had cut the budget by 30% and increased tuition by 20%, which meant I had a 50% loss in my budget. I couldn't continue to give the scholarships and recruit like I had, and it was showing. So that year I didn't recruit any new people except an all-star junior college team. Junior college kids usually need to play three years. You don't want them to play the first year because they've got to get acclimated. They think they can play, but they're playing on a junior college level. When you get to four-year colleges it's a whole lot different. I had the best that we could get, and I sat them out, and let them be the scout team. They were going to be the other folks' team when we practiced, but the public didn't know that. That's where most of the scholarship dollars had gone. Well, it's like they say, you get what you pay for. I was playing primarily with students who were graduating and who had come to school as Physical Education majors but who hadn't made the team so that I could have scholarship money for the next year. Two years after I left, the succeeding coach won the CIAA Tournament Championship. He was a good coach and a personal friend of mine.

At the end of my last tournament, I said, "I just want to let you all know that this is my last game. I am retiring as of this game. And I want to apologize for the way we played today," I said, "because we didn't play well. But it's been a good thirty years. I have enjoyed it, and you've been wonderful. I just want you to be the first to know." They stood up - fourteen thousand people - and they gave me a standing ovation. And I walked on into the sunset. I choked up later, but I was in control that night. I knew it was the right time. The story was all over the six o'clock news.

Money talks: Athletics in the Segregated South

Back in the 60's and the 70's, there were a lot of great black ball players in black colleges. Black colleges were the place to be for athletics at that time. White people would go and see the black teams play, and on New Year's Day when they had the bowl games, the white southern teams who had great records were getting barbecued - Bear Bryant at Alabama and all those schools. But they had no black ball players. The reason that they had great records was they hadn't played the top teams. But that was hype, because you were living in that time and it just wasn't accepted. The black players who could play went to the Midwest, the West coast and up north to Syracuse. They were recruiting these players from the South, but you never heard about them until there were bowl games, because TV games weren't that prevalent either. The only games you really saw were local games and then the bowl games because they were carried by the big networks. People would say, "Well here's Bobby Bell from New Bern, North Carolina," and folks went, "What in the world's he doing out there?" You see, there was a whole lot of money going on, and where they were playing the teams were making money. So they found out that, if we don't have some black ball players, folks wouldn't want to see us play. *You're talking about money. Money's green. Everybody understands money.* So that's when it happened. When it happened in the public schools, there was a lot of money to be made too. Because everybody was playing and at that time there wasn't too much you could go see. But everybody loved to go see the athletic teams. The gyms would just be overflowing. So when they first integrated the schools, they "integrated the schools," but they still had black schools and white schools. The black students who wanted to go to the white schools could go.

The feeling was that there was going to be a big bonanza because the white schools in the South had never played the black schools. They had always been separate. The white press played up how the white teams were going to barbecue the black teams - because that's all they had scouted or seen. They didn't know anything else. Then when they started playing, and they started to have to play "84/32," it was an altogether different ball game. After integration, they took the best black ball players, the best teachers, and the best students and put them in the white schools. That left most of the black schools at a really big disadvantage because white students didn't enroll in black public schools. But we knew that. That's when I retired from high school coaching and went to college. Because I couldn't continue to field the teams that I had been filling with all my players gone. I coached at high school for sixteen years and college for twenty-five years.

When I first graduated from college I coached high school in Clayton, which was my home. I won a state championship there. The first year I coached in Gatesville County we won a championship there. I really loved Clayton, because that was my home, and I knew the kids, their parents, the townsfolk, and for Clayton to win the state championship was just totally unheard of. Not only did I coach the kids but I also taught them. They all had to take my classes, which at that time were algebra, geometry and physics, chemistry, physical education and biology.

You had to teach everything back then, because at that time there weren't a whole lot of teachers. I taught Sunday school; I was Assistant Superintendent; my father was superintendent of Sunday school, so I had them in church too. I had them pretty much all the time. One mama said, "If Coach Heartley were to tell all of them to go run through that wall, they'd do it." I enjoyed them. I played with them, because at that time I was still playing. So I could show them what to do. You know it wasn't a matter of saying it - I could just get out there with you and demonstrate.

My own career saga

When I graduated, I was drafted by the Minneapolis Lakers of the NBA - they're the Los Angeles Lakers now - but they didn't know I was black. They thought I was white. NCCU - NCSU - UNC were often misrepresented. There was no elaborate scouting system for the NBA. We're talking the 50's now; the War was just over. So they had to just listen and see what the things were. We had write ups in the paper just like Duke and Carolina. But when it said North Carolina College, a lot of them thought it was Carolina, or N.C. State. I had good stats, so I was drafted. I didn't even have the money to go to Minneapolis, and besides that, it was cold. I didn't want to go.

I was working in New York with the city of New York as a Physical Activity Director, and I enjoyed that. But I wanted to coach, so I had two contracts to coach in North Carolina. I didn't want my kids to grow up in New York. I wanted them to grow up in my home with my parents and my grandparents. So I left New York and came to Gatesville, NC. I stayed there for a year and then I came to Clayton. I stayed there for about seven years, built a great program, enjoyed all of it. But that was during the time integration was really coming out and Raleigh had a better school system. I thought about the education of my kids. People had wanted me to come to Raleigh, but my kids were not school age at that time. So once they reached school age I just moved to Raleigh and went on at the high school there, which was a very good high school - Ligon High School. I worked there from '64 to '70. Twiggy Sanders, who played with the Globetrotters, went there. I gave him his first basketball. I had some great years - some championship years. I coached football, basketball and tennis. I had four state tennis championships, men and women. After integration, I started losing players.

I went into state government because at that time they were having problems in the school systems with the black kids and white kids fighting. Terry Sanford was governor, and he said he needed somebody who was respected and that the people in the community knew to negotiate racial issues. This was the early 70's. The racial tension was spreading out everywhere in North Carolina. So we developed youth organizations in the schools and communities, and I was the State Youth Coordinator. Then after some success they made me the District Coordinator for the Fifth Congressional District from Virginia all the way down to Florida to Tennessee. But I went to the CIAA tournament, and they were bouncing that ball, and I decided to come back. Everybody said, "Why don't you come back? We need you." In Raleigh, their colleges weren't doing too well, so they wanted me to come back; so that's how I got back into coaching.

At Christmas my first year we were undefeated. I had some veterans and some pretty good players and we did pretty well. My first mistake was when I went to recruit. I didn't recruit kids that were big enough and fast enough to be in the college area. I didn't know too much outside of North Carolina, so far as recruiting, and I tried to recruit in North Carolina. Then I found I had to compete with State, Duke and Carolina. All those kids that I'd coached against, I knew they weren't thinking about coming to St. Augustine's. That reality hit me. They were bigger; they were faster; they were stronger. It takes you a couple of years to find that out. You might have been all right in high school, son; but they'll eat you alive in college.

You have advisors when you go to college. Once you get there and you register, you think you know what you want to do. But then some of you don't. Those that don't go to an "undeclared" advisor, who is usually at the Student Development Center. What they do is advise those youngsters who haven't decided what they want to be. What I tried to do with the athletes that I brought in, for those who didn't know what they wanted to do, was persuade them to go into the Physical Education area, whether they wanted to be teachers, whether they wanted to go to pro, whether they wanted to do physical therapy, or whether they wanted to work with handicapped people. There were a whole lot of things you could do. The reason I did that was because I wanted to teach them, because I wanted to relate what was going on with athletics with what was going on in the classroom. *Also, it let me keep an eye on them in class.*

Career changes

In this time of rapid change, your careers might change two or three times, or you might get tired of what you're doing. But unless you save a lot of money, you have to do something else. So whatever it is that you've developed an interest in, you start to work on that and develop your skills there. Then you make the jump. Or it might be just that you're going to move to another level in the same profession. Rather than being a teacher, you're going to be, say, a supervisor. After you become a supervisor, you might want to be an assistant superintendent. Then you might want to be a superintendent. Or you might want to get out of that field and go into counseling. There are so many things that you might want to do, but you don't need to change until you've thought about it for a while. You always need to really look at the plusses and the minuses. You also need to talk with people who are in the field, because there are a lot of caveats that exist out there that you don't see.

Motivated by money

If a kid tells me he wants to "make a lot of money." I say well, "Who makes a lot of money?" There's nothing wrong with making a lot of money. Money is a great, great medicine for most ills. Everybody should make as much money as they possibly can make. But then you have to learn how to manage the money. I think it's an admirable goal for people to want to make money. We've made money a bad thing. Most of the people I know who have money do good things. Most of the people doing bad things are folks trying to make fast money.

Going back to my philosophy of how to choose a profession, you find out what you really like to do and then get paid for it - for yourself first, then others second. If you can't get paid for what you really want to do, then you have to do what I call "***thrift thinking.***" You have to think, I'd really like to do this, but I don't think I can make enough money at it. But if you think about it, if you're really good at whatever it is you do, you can make a lot of money. I don't care what it is. If you're the garbage man, if you're a good garbage man, people will pay you to come and get their garbage and keep it like it ought to be. I'll just take Tiger Woods, for example. Now all he does is hit a golf ball. You can make a hundred million dollars hitting a golf ball? Now that's probably a little bit way out, but all I'm saying is if you really like it and you're good at it, you can make just as much money as you need. When I say as much money as you need, I don't mean as much as you want, but enough to carry your lifestyle. **Anytime you have enough money to live without having to work, you're rich**. You can't ever get enough to do *everything* you want, but you can get enough. So I would still say do what you want to do with a passion, and get paid. Now if you can't do that, then find out how you can get paid and stay in that job long enough to put yourself in a situation where you don't have to do it again if you don't like it. I think the bottom line is, **if you really want to do something, you're going to get paid for it**.

You can be **whatever** you are willing to **WORK** to be.

Some things to do.

IX. <u>**PROFESSIONAL MATTERS:**</u>

1. Write out honestly what profession you would passionately like to pursue.

2. Write out the assets and skills you possess that would make you a success in that profession.

3. Seek the advice of a **successful person** in that profession.

4. Write out a plan for pursuing your professional choice or choices.

5. Go to the library. Talk with the librarians. Get on-line. Do research.

6. Find a <u>good</u> <u>COACH</u>.

7. Do what <u>you</u> want to do!

POLITICAL MATTERS

Define it first

According to the dictionary, politics is "the art or science of guiding and influencing policies." Of course, you're never supposed to use the word to define itself. I look at it as *competition between people, groups, or individuals for power, control and leadership*. Politics started with Adam, Eve and the serpent in the negotiation of the apple, if you believe that story. There were three people vying for power, control and leadership. God supposedly gave the control to Adam and the "followship" to Eve. *If you have a leader you also have to have followers*. In any political relationship, you have to answer this question: *who's going to do the leading and who's going to do the following?*

Politics at home

Politics starts in the home, between husband and wife in deciding who wants to assume the leadership, the power, the control. We're going through some trying times now because, in the Southern Baptist church, in the Muslim religion and a lot of other man/wife religious situations, we're trying to say that men have a certain place and women have a certain place. I think people do have places. It doesn't matter whether you're a man or a woman. If we're trying to do what is best for the body politic, then the leadership will depend upon who can get the group's goals accomplished, be they male or female. Because traditionally men have been the "leaders," they often assume that they have all it takes to be the leaders, and that is questionable. When I taught mathematics and courses that were analytical, the women often were way ahead of the men, but sometimes they would not let on. When I read the papers and corrected them, though, I knew who knew what was going on, and I encouraged them. Even way back in the 50's, I told them that there's no

215

corner on mentality, there's no
corner on brains. I read the book <u>Men</u>
<u>Are From Mars, Women From Venus</u>, and
I'm happy to say that I never had
those problems because we had an
egalitarian family. My mom and father
ruled together. If there were
conflicts, my mother would defer to
my father - not necessarily because
she thought that he had more sense,
but because we were brought up in a
traditional Christian family, and my
grandparents were of the opinion that
the man ruled the house. The women
had input, but if it came down to one
person's way, it usually was the
man's way. But he had a
responsibility then, because if it
broke down, that was his problem.
With choices come consequences. So if
we go with your choice, you deal with
the consequences. They usually talked
things out. Not only do you have the
politics going on between the adults,
but children also act politically
because they try from day one to
manipulate the parents. They'll cry.
They'll want to be picked up. We had
a rule in our house that if a child
was well, didn't have a temperature,
was dry and fed, we let him or her
cry. It helps develop their lungs and

vocal chords. Parents need to have some strategy like that because children will learn how to manipulate you by figuring out what it is that makes you vulnerable. **Whether you think you're in the political arena or not, you're in one**, and it starts at home. **You need to be aware.**

Community politics

If you aren't careful, you'll be persuaded by the thoughts of the people in your community, because they want you to do what they want you to do. They will control your mind, too, and if you don't go along with them, they will put sanctions on you to let you know that your thoughts are not the thoughts of the group. You have to be careful about that. So what you have to know is: how do I act? What type of leadership do I want to bring to the table? **Do I want to lead or do I want to follow?** I find that the people who want to lead are not always the people who should be doing the leading. Often the people who are following are doing so mainly because they have looked a step beyond where the ones who want to lead are, and they don't

217

think that, in the long run, they want to put up with all of the issues that are out there. I believe politics in itself is a very noble profession. I was in politics for one year, and I knew that I was not going to make a very good politician. I could have if I had wanted to compromise some of my integrity, and if I had wanted to let my ego get the better of me. I just didn't think that compromising my integrity was healthy for me.

Making a difference as an individual

To live our political lives effectively, we need to be productive and to help influence the family, the community, the faith community, our businesses or corporations, and our political parties. We need to be able to bring something to the table, and usually that means some **time, energy, money, skills, and other resources like facilities**. Those are the things you look at when you're bringing help to a political arena. Often people don't know what they bring to the table, but they want to take a lot off the table. If we're going to prepare the table such that everybody is going to eat, then somebody has to prepare that food. *Now, if you're eating, at some point you need to bring something of value to the table*. You can't just always pull your chair up. That's the way I used to talk to my basketball teams: "Son, you know, we want you to play, we want you to be in there, but you've got to bring something to the table. You know you have to make a contribution."

In the community, we speak of it as *civic responsibility*. Most of the time when people think about politics, they think about the Democratic Party and the Republican Party, and who's mayor, etc., but if we each think about doing something to help people, then we become in essence mini-leaders ourselves by realizing that we have a responsibility to do something. I was listening to the presidential debates last year, and the morning after one debate, I heard Tom Joyner do a critique of it. The Tom Joyner show is a nationally syndicated FM radio show with a primarily black listening audience. That morning, Tom said, "Well neither one of you guys touched on any of the black issues. What about HIV/AIDS? What about inner city growth? What about affirmative action?" He pointed out strongly that black people had an agenda too; and he had Gore on the phone the next night. Tom Joyner has substantial influence with black voters, so he's going to be a factor in the political arena. But then I take it a step farther. I say, *if we know what's important and what needs to be done, then why don't we do it?* If these are the things that affect us, then certainly the government should help. They have resources; but we have resources too. When I say "we," I'm not necessarily talking about black people. I'm talking about "we" collectively. Some people think about white people, black people, Asian people, etc.; I say *we're all people. Your problem is my problem, and my problem is your problem.* Most people don't look down the line and anticipate. *The natural order of things says, if it's going to affect me, eventually it's going to affect you too.* So I need to get it straight with you before it jumps over on me. That's what happened with Hitler and Milesovic, and all those people who let others take advantage of them without anybody saying anything and doing something about it. *If they take advantage of you, they'll take advantage of me and vice versa.* You have to look at it from that standpoint.

Political parties

I've been a Democrat for a long time, and I probably will continue to be one because I think that it has shown that it's the best party for those people who are concerned about the majority of people. I have nothing against the Republican Party if they have ideas and actions that respond to issues affecting the majority of the people.

There's always going to be a problem between Republicans and Democrats because there are always going to be differences among people on many fronts. The things that rich people want are probably not going to be the same things that poor people want, but I think there has to be a happy medium in there somewhere. Bush talked about big tax cuts. Gore said Bush was going to give it to the rich people. I think somewhere down the line, the rich people ought to get some money, and the poor people too. It doesn't have to be an "either/or" scenario. *I always say it's "either/or/and."* It took me a long time to learn that you don't always have to choose one or the other; often you can have both. That's the paradox of living. In some instances, the two sides look like they're diametrically opposed, but in reality they are not. A good leader is one who is able to identify some core things that would be fair to the rich, some to the middle class, some to the poor, and what's ultimately going to be best for the majority of the people for a long time.

Politics in the church

Right now there is a split politically in the church. The Southern Baptists are stating that they don't necessarily want women in the pulpit, and that the duty of the wife is to follow the husband. I don't have any problem with that if that's the way they want it, but from an egalitarian standpoint, I don't think it's a good thing. *I've known a lot of women with much more leadership ability and skills than most men*, and that's a big source of problems that have come up within the churches and other organizations. As I have taught relationships in college, I have gotten a pretty good idea about what a male wants and what a female wants, and usually they're not too different. In class I made the males take the females' role – and the female take the male role in role-playing scenarios. It got uncomfortable because they had to *try to prove a situation* that they were not necessarily in agreement with. That's when their feelings would come in. Logic is one thing, but emotions are something else.

Social habits are also a strong influence on people. When you put somebody in another situation and say, now you've got to argue the ladies' side, they say, "What do you mean?" Both genders usually struggle with the exercise. Eventually, though, everybody gets a better view and a better grasp of how the others feel, and oftentimes how selfish their own desires are. In the Muslim faith, women cannot do certain things. In fact, I don't know of any religion where the women are in charge and they tell the men that they can't do certain things. There might be one, but I don't know of any.

I believe that the politics that exists between individuals should be the same politics that exists within organizations. In business, women make only about 75% of the money that men make, and there are glass ceilings that prevent them from getting the highest-level positions. I think all that should change, but I'm not in that arena. I know that some men have a difficult time taking orders from women. Why, I don't know, but they do. I've seen it in organizations. The mere fact that the woman is running something, all of a sudden she isn't qualified in the eyes of the men – even if she's got a PhD in Administration. She's working for the corporation, so what do you mean she can't run it? We have to break those walls down.

Politics defined by culture

Certain beliefs are instilled in you because you had to take on the culture in which you lived. Perhaps the culture in which you live said that this is a man's world, and people believed that, but **America was settled and developed by both men and women.** The reason that women have as much freedom in America as they do is because they were out there defending their families, cutting trees down, and growing food too. They have just as much right as the men do, if you just think about it. But many people don't want to look at it. They don't want to be bothered by the facts and the truth; they just want what they want. When you sit down and look at the literature, you have to realize that the literature sometimes is biased too. So when you look, you have to look at all of the literature, not just selected literature. I wouldn't say the textbooks are necessarily inaccurate, but they give you a frame of reference.

History is just what it says: "His story." You can't prove most of it. The Bible was written hundreds of years after Christ. Most people can't remember what happened last year. Can you imagine trying to write a book hundreds of years after the events happened? So you have to look at things with a grain of salt. Then again, the Bible is a history of the Jewish leaders and their people. It isn't a history of all mankind. The world was still going on. Most of the time it was the leaders, the kings, the scribes, the lawyers, those people who wrote books, so you have to look at everything within the context of how things were at the time.

Lessons about politics

My overall message to readers is that, *in every aspect of your life, you've got to know that politics exists*. You need to get involved and make a difference; you need to make sure you do not compromise your integrity. *There are two things that you don't want to do: compromise your integrity and let your ego get out of control.* I've found that sometimes people get into positions of leadership because they want all the prestige and perks that go with the job. Then when they get there, a lot of them get into what I call the "leadership trap." They realize that it's not what they really want to do, but people want them to continue. People always want you to continue. They want you to do all the work and solve all the problems, and if it doesn't work then they'll say, "See, I knew he wasn't the right leader to start with." Now you're talking politics.

The political arena can make some people intoxicated with power. They have the people, the tax base, money and other resources. They have the approval of at least one group, and once they get in there, they just don't want to leave. The first Continental Congress was not that way. We were supposed to go there in the spring, have a little meeting, find out what was going on, what was needed, make appropriations, and then go back home. Then they started raising taxes and they got D.C. laid out. It got to be nice, and they said, "Hey, I could get used to this." It's intoxicating. Once they get in, they don't want to leave. I'm not saying that you have to leave, or that getting intoxicated with it is bad. *I think it's bad if you are not doing the will of the people.*

Developing future leaders

I think there should be time limits on all positions of power because, although you might be doing a great job, *the purpose* of the leadership is *to develop competent followers who will eventually replace you.* Most people want to lead and keep everybody else down, but my true definition of a leader is one who develops future leaders along the way. As a teacher, I didn't want to develop followers or just college graduates. *I was trying to develop leaders.* I tried to develop all my students to be leaders. I knew all of them were not going to be leaders, but they had to be subjected to the leadership atmosphere to find out what it was about so they'd have a better appreciation of the people who did lead. You'll be a better follower if you have tried to be a leader, if that's what you wanted to do.

"BUPDL" leadership

There are a number of different leadership styles: autocratic, democratic, monocratic, laissez faire, etc. Mine is what I call **"BUPDL": "Bottoms Up, Participatory, Democratic Leadership."** It's a method that gives everybody in the group the responsibility to bring something to the table. Some people are going to bring more than others, but the group decides for the group what's the best thing. It doesn't mean yours was bad. We've got a record of it because, although it might not be good now, two or three years from now, it might be pertinent. But we know where it is. I think it's sort of sad that we only have two candidates that people say are capable of leading the country. I know that's not true. You've got to raise one hundred million dollars to run for president. I don't know how you're going to get around money. **Money is a hard thing to get around - in politics or in any other aspect of life.** Normally, the more money that goes to an aspect of living, the better it gets if the plan was a good one, the better your life processing will be - all things

229

being equal. ***Money is simply stored work***. If you've got money in the bank, you had to get that money some kind of way, most likely through some type of work. Then you stored it (saved and invested it) so that you could reuse it. There's a book called The Psychology of Money that I would recommend to readers. It shows how people react to money and how certain things are processed psychologically because of money.

There's also a book called Sexual Politics that deals with the politics of gender, and because you've got men and women who are always in some type of political situation, you need to be aware of it to know if it's being used on you. You can go to any good library or to the internet to find material on politics. ***If you really want to do something, you can do it. It's just a matter of your doing it. Just be what you want to be. Behave that way.***

Some things to do.

X. **POLITICAL MATTERS:**

1. Get yourself and all family members that are 18 years old and older registered to vote.

2. Schedule a meeting with your voter precinct chairperson.

3. Attend the next precinct meeting with your eligible family members.

4. Volunteer to become a block chairperson.

5. Register with the political party of your choice.

6. Go to the library. Talk with the librarians. Get on-line. Do research.

7. Find a <u>good</u> <u>COACH</u>.

8. Do what <u>you</u> want to do!

SEXUALITY

What do we mean?

Without sexuality, the human race or any species would cease to exist. Webster defines sexuality as "relating to or involving sex, or the sexes." When I use the term sexuality, I want to include sensuality also. To be sensual means that we're relating to gratification of the senses, or the physical pleasures related to the senses or sex. So when we say a person is sexual, we're not necessarily saying that the person is sensual.

We are all sexual beings. We manifest our sexuality in different ways, but we're born either male or female biologically. That's what I call the plumbing, the equipment. How we are raised determines our gender because, although you may be born a male, you may have female tendencies. And although you are born female, you might have male tendencies. From a biological standpoint, until the first six weeks in the development of the fetus, everybody is thought to be female. Whether the sex cells develop into ovaries or whether they develop into testes depends upon a hormonal makeup of testosterone and estrogen and the other sex hormones that determine what your sex is going to be.

From the standpoint of men who are gay, there could be a biological explanation having to do with the sex hormones. Whether you are male or female is decided within your brain. The brain has to make that decision as to what you are. (**These are my theories**.) It might happen that the signal is sent to the chromosomes or the genes for you to have the sex organs of a male, but in the brain (due to hormonal mix-ups or faulty chemical imbalances) it's determined or deciphered as female. This means that there is possibly a biological error that explains why a man can be born gay. A female is a little bit different because all females who are born female are always going to have the sexual organs of a female. They are never going to develop a penis. In the mind, in the brain, the brain chemistry might just secrete or give the genes the recognition that you're a male, but the equipment is female.

We see aberrations in everything. Things change. All trees are not the same trees. All squirrels are not the same squirrels. So it's clear that nature makes mistakes also, and that's when we get into some situations wherein people may not know whether they are male or female.

I think parents should know these things, and so should the faith communities. I don't think we should make judgments about people's sexuality. These things start at an early age because youngsters will explore their genitalia, and often we'll slap them on the hand and admonish them at an age when they don't know what they're doing. They do that because research shows that it's pleasurable and they're exploring (unknowingly) their sexuality. Somewhere in their life it's developing their sexuality, and we shouldn't be unduly concerned about that.

The responsibilities of parenthood

When you bring somebody into the world, you have to think about the fact that *you're going to be his or her parents forever*. That concept might be a little foreign to people, and it might be a little bit way out. A young parent may say, "When he gets to be eighteen . . . I'll be so glad when he gets to be eighteen," but that's not the point. The philosophy of parenthood is that you're bringing somebody into the world that you might have to take care of for life because he or she might be born with a disability or defect. So don't think that you're going to be absolved of your parental responsibilities when they get to be eighteen. *You're their parents for as long as you live*, and as long as you can help them, I think you have a moral obligation to do so. Your responsibility never ends. So *we need to be very careful about bringing youngsters into the world*.

To ensure that they maintain good health, you need to look at *prevention, education, treatment and rehabilitation*. The first aspect to address is the upfront prevention. You need to know what's going on in the sexual arena. You also need to know what will be going on when you decide that you want to have sex with someone, and at what age that should

235

happen. When youngsters reach the age of puberty, they should know about it. The parents should know about it. In some states, parents have to decide whether their children get sex education in school or not. It's not taught as a basic subject, but children can take it *ex officio* if their parents sign a statement. In reality, it's the parents who sometimes aren't comfortable and who probably aren't doing a good job talking about it at home.

Most churches don't want to talk about it either. Sex and procreation are the basis for all life. You cannot skirt around that. As a parent, you have to sit down with your children and talk about it. Not only that, **you have to know what you're talking about.** Questions are going to come up, so you need to know beforehand what the questions are and what the answers are. The answers come from the literature, the experts, and the faith community. They also come from your faith, and often, the two are contradictory.

It's not by accident that nature has made it possible for the human race to reproduce at a very early age: ten, eleven, twelve. The reason for that is that in an agricultural, agrarian economy, we need as many people to till the land and share the work responsibility as possible. When I was talking about creativity and imagination, I said that God left a lot of the imagination to us, but in the grand scheme of things, He thought it was in the best interest of man to be able to reproduce at an early age. *God gave us choices; He didn't give us answers*.

If you go back to the Natural Order Of Things-- (*N.O.O.T.*), and the way that we lived in the past, the children came up within a social community, waiting for somebody to teach them. The people best prepared to teach youngsters how to live are the grandparents and the elders. The young people, the parents, at that age, don't know how a child should be raised. The only thing they know is how to *have* them. They need to be working to help provide for the elderly people who may no longer be able to do daily physical work.

We have choices, and society has decided that young people shouldn't have sex because it creates too many problems: social problems, emotional problems, sexually transmitted disease problems, etc. Yes, that's true. But the body says it wants sex, so you've got a conflict. *Remember that life is all a paradox*. So, in our infinite wisdom, we have to figure out a way that is best for us. What works best for our community? Is ignorance of sexual matters best, or is intelligence best? Inasmuch as God gave everybody the ability to choose, you can't protect the kids forever. You have to let them know the facts of life. You have to let them know where you stand. Let them know what you think is in their best interest and the best interest of the family and the community, and then the choice is left to them. But in case they err, *they should know what safe sex means*. I believe we should teach young people about contraceptive products - birth control pills, condoms, etc. - all of the things that will keep them from getting into a situation that we know they can't handle. As parents, we should let them know the psychological effects of early sex. Not necessarily the morality implications, because the definition of morality changes. We can't legislate morality; but when you've been intimate with another person, there are certain spiritual and emotional feelings that are going to exist. They won't necessarily exist forever, but we know biologically that they will exist for four to six years. Then after that, it dwindles, and for each life passage that you go through, the sexuality and the sensuality change. Over time, the endorphins are not jumping up and down like they were in the beginning. That kind of romantic love is not going to last forever. As you grow through your 20's, 30's, 40's, 50's, 60's, 70's, and 80's, certain things are going to happen to you sexually and in each other aspect of your life. You have to know that these things will occur beforehand and make plans for the time they arrive.

Sexual politics

Sexual politics means that some people will use sex to get their way. You have to be aware of that because it exists in the family between husband and wife. There are certain roles that men think wives should play, and there are certain roles that wives think men should play. You can go to the literature and see what the majority of the people think, which doesn't really mean anything, but at least you know the mind set of the community and your environment. You really have to sit down and talk that situation out with your spouse or with your "significant other." You should be open about those things because your philosophy might be diametrically opposed to that of the other person.

Some people are just sensual by nature. They're easygoing; they're easy to get along with, and there's just something about them that seems to attract people. They don't necessarily have to be beautiful or rich, but they have something that we call *"class." Class is not the school you went to; it's not the car you drive; it's not the clothes you wear. Class either Is or it Isn't. You can't buy it. You can't beg it. "Class simply is."* People with class don't have to say anything. They don't have to do anything. They don't have to come in wearing a mink coat, but there's always a presence when they are around - an aura. *It makes you just smile to yourself.*

Sexual philosophy

There are basically four primary reasons for sex: there's sex for **pleasure**, sex for **procreation**, sex for **money**, and sex for **political reasons**. I've found in my life that men and women have sex for different reasons. Most men have sex because they are biologically predisposed to have sex. The more women that men have sex with and have children with, the more their genes are dispersed such that we will have a wider variety of people with, hopefully, different positive traits. Testosterone is more prevalent in men than in women. Most men have sex and then fall in love after the fact. Most women fall in love first and then have sex.

I think women are by nature predisposed to look for a man who can protect and provide for them and their children, because biologically they know that there's going to come a time when they're not going to be able to provide for themselves (during pregnancy and immediately after childbirth). So over the years nature and evolution have said to the woman, "Before you can go out here and try to have pleasure and spread your seed like a man, you have to think about whether you're going to survive, and whether your offspring are going to survive." So women tend to delay and try to find those traits in a man that they can feel comfortable with, and feel belonging to, and being cared for, because they know that eventually they're going to have children if they have sex.

We had no birth control products in the natural order of things (**N.O.O.T.**), but through the years, they have been developed and they enable women now to look around until they find someone they really like – someone they are comfortable with and that they believe will take good care of them and their children - they then decide they love him and they're ready to have his kids.

So in recent years we have been biologically predisposed in a different manner. Society says it's best for you to have one spouse, or one mate. That's in the western world. In some countries, a man can have up to four wives, legally, if he can support them, and there's an order to that. But in America, we said, "No, you can't do that." So what you have is married men who might have mistresses, and wives who want to hold their husbands to their wedding vows, and it's embarrassing if that doesn't happen. So we have to think about those things too. There again, it's in the contract that exists between the two consenting people. *We don't have answers; we have choices, and all choices are paradoxical; consequences follow choices.*

Every individual has to develop his or her own philosophy on sensuality and sexuality. As you get older, your philosophies will change based on experiences, the situations and your age.

It's up to parents to prepare their children for the sexual choices they will have to make, because the school and the church are not ultimately responsible to deal with the subject. So it has to be addressed with the parents, the grandparents and within the family. *Children usually do what you do.* You can talk all you want to, but they watch, and they see the love and affection that is shown between the family members. I would like to see a lot of talk about this subject, but most people are afraid to talk about it.

I talked to my children about it at an early age. My wife and I were prepared for it. We let our daughters know that there were going to be menstrual periods, and we let our son know that when it came along, although he didn't have a period, his sisters were going to be having them and what the process was. I taught biology and physical education; I coached girls and boys, and I knew when they had periods. I knew better than they did. If you've been honest and fair with your kids from day one, and you know how you want to raise them, you won't have trouble talking to them. If you don't talk to them, they will get their information from others, and then they'll get distortions and misinformation.

The ignorance out there on this subject is astronomical. I taught sex education to freshmen in a wellness class, and the ideas that they came in with were amazing to say the least. They didn't even know about their own anatomy, much less the anatomy of the other person. They didn't know about the biological phases that their bodies would be going through. When parents talk to their children about these things, they have to be knowledgeable themselves. **You can't teach what you don't know.**

The thought police

The thought police are thinking taboos that society has put on us. There are certain sexual things that you don't do; don't even think about. A guy just can't get into ladies' clothes and walk down the street. You have what they call kinky sex – sodomy, oral sex. Most of these acts are on the books as being crimes against nature. There are certain things that certain religions tell you that you cannot do in a sexual realm. In any type of sexual relationship, I think it should be left up to the two consenting adult individuals. In some states, however, that can get you twenty years in jail.

A developing philosophy about it is **if it doesn't hurt anyone, if it's discreet, and if it's between consenting adults, then it's okay.** There is nothing taboo. **There is** *nothing that can't be examined*. Think about it and come up with your own conclusions. Identify the worst-case scenarios. What is the worst thing that can happen if you think about this happening? What you find out is that you grow. You cannot have infinite processing if you've got thought police and you're stuck within the box. *You can't be afraid to think outside the box*.

We're always trying to look for truth, whatever it is. Truth changes too. As our ability to interpret things evolves, we find that what was true twenty years ago is not true now. We've taken it to another level, and that's the way you want to live your life. *Every day you get up, you know that something new is happening*. Something else is out there to be created, and you're going to have fun creating in all of the various aspects of your life. Creating is a most pleasurable adventure.

Wherever your passions lie, that's what you should do. You owe it to yourself to *be sensual*. You owe it to yourself to *be attractive*. You owe it to yourself to be able to *give pleasure*. You owe it to yourself to be able to *receive pleasure*. You should always **be discreet**. That's basically a philosophy. I have not tried to give people answers; I've tried to make them think. I've just given people what's out there. They have to find the answers for themselves, but they also have to realize that there's a paradox because there aren't many everlasting answers. There are just choices, and after you've made those choices you have to evaluate them to see if they were in your best interest, or were they in somebody else's best interest. **I always like win-win situations**.

Now when you get to lifestyles in the sexual realm, you have a movement going on concerning gay and lesbian couples getting health care and other workers' social benefits. You also have lesbian couples adopting or having babies, and older women having children through in vitro fertilization and embryo implantation. All of this raises questions such as when two lesbians raise a male child, how do they teach him how to be male? Or if two gay men want to raise a child, a girl or a boy, how do they relate to that child in their sexuality and their sensuality? These are problems that are going to exist. Most everybody's family (if you want to look in the closet) over time has this problem one way or the other. Now I won't say it's a problem, but we have this situation and we have to ask ourselves, is it in some ways part of the natural order of things?

Nature versus nurture

We also have theories about what we call environment and heredity. You inherit some traits. You are predisposed genetically to certain things. What happens when you have that situation and there are youngsters being raised? For instance, if the mother is a truck driver and the husband is a househusband, and he decides that he wants to stay home and take care of the kids and the wife goes off to work. Let's say, for argument's sake, that they have a boy and a girl. How does that play out in the personalities and tendencies of the children? Will the little boy be more domestic? Will the girl be like her mother and take a more traditionally male-oriented career path? All of these things have to be thought about when you choose your style of living, and these are some questions that I don't think government or laws will be able to answer. I think it depends upon the individuals. **Laws will go on the books to regulate behavior** because that's why we have statutes and laws - to protect the rights of the individual, and to protect the rights of groups. That is determined in a court of law.

Spiritual Sex

There are different levels of what I call sexiness, and some of it is for pleasure, some is for procreation, and then there's what we call "spiritual sex." **Spiritual sex is when you know that you're going to a place that only the two of you can go**, and **you've never been there and are not likely to go with anybody else**. Bells ring and chimes peal, and you just know that this is how it should be. It doesn't get any better than that. That's why we call our partner our "soul mate". That doesn't mean that he or she's going to be your only soul mate, or that it's going to feel that way all the time, but at least it lets you know what's possible. **Unless you know what's possible, you might think what you've got is good**. There are all levels and the levels never end. **Infinite processing. Infinite sexuality.**

SOME THINGS TO DO.

XI. SEXUALITY:

1. Assess your sex life with your partner.

2. Are there problems in your sex life?

3. Talk with your sexual partner about how he/she evaluates your satisfaction.

4. Write out and practice ways you can enhance your sex life.

5. Think of ways in which you can discuss your sexual philosophy with your children and write them down. *

6. Go to the library. Talk with the librarians. Get on-line. Do research.

7. Find a <u>good</u> <u>COACH</u>.

8. Do what <u>you</u> want to do!

* **Very important.**

SPIRITUALITY

According to Webster

Webster's definition of spirituality is "relating to, consisting of, or affecting the spirit; relating to sacred matters". It's a religious feeling that originates out of the unknown. The experts who are spiritual leaders go a little further than Webster in defining it. They deal with an essence of life that is ethereal - it cannot be felt, it's not tangible, but it exists. I'm going to look at it from that perspective also, but I'd like to make it a little bit personal. *My own definition of spirituality is that we are all one*. We must go back to the beginning. Usually when I speak of something, *I always try to go back to the N.O.O.T.: The time when there was nothing* - that didn't exist before we were physical, before we were mental, and before we were spiritual. *Through some phenomenon, the universe was created.* I'm not trying to define that. I'm not saying I know what that is. I know that I

252

exist in a physical form, but I also think I exist in a spiritual form, and I think that spiritual form is in the essence of what I call **"God," and what was, is, and always will be**. I'm not sure that what we call physical is physical in the perfect sense of physicality. We might be in a spiritual form in another realm acting out those spiritual ideas in the only way that we can - physically on earth. I know that's a little "way out," but somewhere in a spiritual form, I believe I exist. I also exist in a physical form, but the spirit cannot act out because, as my principal used to say, "It has no arms or legs." But I do. When you think about the fact that we're living here on a big ball in the middle of nowhere, spinning around in the universe - it's mind-blowing because when you think about it, it has to be from some phenomenon that is not human. That is what I call "God." That is what I call spirituality. I don't think we'll ever fully understand it, but you can get close and closer so that you can live with it. So when I speak of spirituality, that is the realm in which I'm speaking. *The spiritual manifests the physical.*

All of life is a paradox

You have to come up with your own philosophy of what spirituality is. How do you explain your existence? How do you communicate with the infinite being or infinite spirituality? That's up to you. You either believe it or you don't believe it, which brings us to what I call the *Universal Paradox*: *All of life is a paradox*. You've got to be able to look at two diametrically opposing views and realize that, in certain instances, they both may be right. I know that's inconsistent with our mathematical logic and theory, but I've found, as I've talked to people, as I've studied, as I've lived, that there are some things that transcend logic. With the type of rationale that you could probably use mathematically and theoretically to prove God exists or spirituality exists, you could probably take that same point and turn it around and prove that they do not exist. *So it comes down to a*

254

matter of faith in what you believe.
I believe faith is (ecclesiastically) proof - not proof, but belief in things unseen. There's an old proverb that says, *"Faith is believing in something that does not exist until it does exist."* I think that, from a spiritual realm to a physical realm, you first think about something, and after you've thought about it, you speak it or you write it. If you can believe that, you'll find a way to make that actually exist because *I believe the purpose_of living is to create things from a spiritual realm to a physical realm*. At one time, before creation, nothing except GOD existed. If we can get over the idea of earthly beginnings and endings, it's not too difficult to conceptualize. It's abstract. Get away from beginnings and endings and go to the fact that these things can happen because of your thought processes. *"Everything is created out of thought*, and *if you can think it, you can write it, you can say it, and you can believe it, then it can occur."*

I don't think there are many impossibilities - though there may be improbabilities. We simply are

255

limited in our thoughts and our creative abilities to make things happen. I think that we will always exist, we have always existed, and we probably will always exist as long as we **think** we will.

In order to grow spirituality, you have to have ideas and concepts. Usually that's brought about in the home, the school, the church, and the neighborhood. Those concepts are passed down from the parents as part of the culture or heritage. I'm not speaking about spirituality from the standpoint of the church, or the synagogue, or the tabernacle. I'm talking about individual spirituality that exists primarily between you and the spiritual world, which I will call God, or you can call Allah or whomever. *There first has to be a one-on-one relationship between you and whomever you choose as your spiritual mentor*. You have to be taught at an early age about certain things that exist in the culture because, if not, you won't have a frame of reference to turn to once you run into problems.

When you are young, you are probably indoctrinated into certain faiths because that's where you live.

You had no choice. But as you get older and you read and you think and you interact with people who are of different faiths, you see some good things and some things that you question. Ultimately, it all becomes a matter of that last definition: **what is it that you believe? What is it that you know deep down without coercion from the "thought police"?** When you think out of the box, and when you're allowed to think freely, without any fear, punishment, heresy or insecurity, just what have you found to be truth? You have to seek your own, because you cannot be really healthy until you do seek. Once you find it, you can still experience those things within the church and other faith-based organizations that you participate in because **we are social beings**. You should understand that, within the context of those things, there are going to be some things that you don't believe in. I'm not saying that you should point that out to people because they have to find their own truth, but I think, spiritually, you have to have that conversation in the morning, in the afternoons, with your "other self" - perhaps your alter ego. I don't know who or what it is, but when I start to talk spiritually and to meditate, somehow or other I'm into contact with another realm of my being. I'm not saying that anybody else would find that; I'm just saying try it sometime. I'm not trying to give answers or to prove anything. I'm not trying to indoctrinate anybody in any way, I'm just trying to say *be truthful to yourself*; realize that you didn't create this, and ask yourself how you can reconcile the fact that it exists.

What is your spiritual philosophy?

You have to have some kind of philosophy (a series of basic beliefs that you value and use for guidance) on the subject. And if that makes you happy and comfortable, fine. But as you grow older, you're going to find that, through "infinite processing," as soon as you reach a certain point, another idea is going to pop up and you're going to feel uncomfortable again. So you've got to continue resolving. That's what life is. Every individual has to define his or her own spirituality and philosophy about a Supreme Being, spiritual force, or those things that you can't explain or control, and if you can get in touch with that, it adds a richness to your life.

We all have philosophies (whether we know it or not), but what is yours grounded on? Usually a philosophy first should be grounded on what I call universal truths: what is good for everybody on the earth? Then ask yourself what the experts say. Then examine your community; and then go within yourself, because you've got to interact with all of the above. You've got the family to deal with; you've got the community to deal with; you have the social order or the state; and you have the universal law realm to deal with.

You have to look at it from all four standpoints because, usually, if you deal with the universal philosophy, it will serve most everybody best. Then when you go to the national or statewide level, it will be for those particular people, and then when you get to your community and your family, it takes in a smaller number of people. Hopefully we should be able to see how we function in each one of those categories because, in some instances, you'll find that you agree with this particular group but you don't agree with another group.

Your philosophy may change depending on who you are and where you are, but you should have a core philosophy that you believe in, and that should be something that you've looked at from the personal, the international, the national, the local, and the community scenes. From these, you have crafted a philosophy, realizing that as you go out into other realms, your basic philosophy wouldn't change, but you will be better able to understand where other philosophies are coming from. There needs to be a fair amount of tolerance in recognizing that *everybody has a potentially different philosophy*.

Usually if you define what's really best, it's what's best for everybody. But you are not living for everybody. You have certain things that you have to deal with and you have to reconcile those things. *The main purpose of this book is to get people to think about where they're coming from*. First, to define where they're coming from, and then to look at these aspects of their philosophies.

Take time to think about it

Today, people are so busy - technology has moved everything so fast that everybody's flying on the highways or e-mailing, and very seldom do you get the time. But I take the time, at night and in the morning. - when I go to bed and when I wake up - to just put everything from the day in perspective and just think about it. It takes you about fifteen to thirty minutes to go to sleep. During that time you can just meditate on the various aspects of your life to see what happened that day that was good, what was bad, what you should have done, what you didn't do. Think about it and talk with whoever your spiritual being is (I usually use the word "God" because that's inclusive in my culture).

That's the way I was brought up. When you're thinking back about the events of the day, remember that **everything bad that happens to you is not bad for you. It's to teach you a lesson or to steer you onto another**

path. So you think of setbacks and defeats as ways in which you need to learn more. Look at them as chances to improve, not things that are detrimental. Often when I start off the day and it's really going badly - things are not going right, and then I get flustered - then I start the day over. I just wipe that day off and say, "All right, the new day starts today at 2:00 P.M. Forget all that other stuff! I'm starting a new day." *I'll start a new day any time I feel like it! THINK - ADJUST - ADAPT AND MOVE ON!*

Growth is hard

Learning is not necessarily comfortable. Any growth or learning experience is going to be somewhat uncomfortable or threatening. I have a little acronym, *"CSE," that stands for "comfortable, simplistic efficiency,"* which means that you can't daily put in let's say twelve or fourteen hours if you're just on the run - here, there, everywhere. You have to find a level of comfortableness and it's not the same every day. Some days you can do more, some days you can't. But once you reach a point wherein you have sustained "uncomfortable ness," you're going to suffer from stress and burn out or have a breakdown.

You have to work comfortably, and then you have to **simplify what you're doing**. When I say simplify, I don't mean it'll be simplistic, but it will be such that you're doing the best that you can to make it clear to everybody.

Then you want it to **be efficient**. You don't want to spend a lot of energy on something and find out you could have done it a little bit better. I want it to be as efficient as it possibly can be.

As far as change is concerned, I think we should welcome change because **everything changes**. Every day it's a different world. When you wake up the next morning, **God is constantly creating. The earth is moving. The universe is expanding.** It's not the same universe. New things are being created. We're finding new planets. **God is a creating God**, and He/She continuously changes. She/He changes in nanoseconds. We're that way, too. We want to reach a level of comfort and then that's it. We want to get a work philosophy where we can feel comfortable. Well that's all right too, if that's where you want to go, but you will find that there are always questions. ***God gave us choices; He/She didn't give us answers***. That's why you have so many different religions and ways of life, because everybody has choices. That's what makes America so great. We have choices. You put choices and freedom together and you've got the ideal society. That's why so many people are trying to get over here. I think that we should welcome creativity. We should welcome change. It doesn't mean that we're always looking for it. But if you look at what you did during the day when you go to bed at night, you can improve tomorrow. If it bothers you, you can improve or you can stay right where you are. I'm not saying that you have to continue to create, but ***God creates through us because God doesn't have any arms and legs***.

Everything that's going to be created here is going to have to be done by us. I think that ***creativity is the real essence of being***. You're creating yourself right now, just like I'm creating myself, and the more you come in contact with different people and different things, the better person you can create for yourself.

A never-ending cycle

I don't think creation ends. This is an eternal game. I think I will come back again, again and again, as many times as I choose to. I will assume another body. Maybe I will go to another level of physical being, but I don't think that I will ever cease to be a person unless I choose to. I think that if I should choose that – I say, "Well, I want to stop here. I want to stay in my spiritual realm, and I don't want to take on a physical presence." See how infinite choice is?

The mere fact that we can do something, we can experience what we are thinking, I think that's what makes the spiritual and the physical and the mental and all these other realms real or dynamic. *It's a game. It's a never-ending game*. It's one that you can do because that's what you think you can do. *My thoughts are just as good as anybody else's. Who can tell me what I can think? I have free thought, and free mind, and free will.* So if I think this, who's to tell me that I'm wrong? If I want to live forever, then I'll live forever. When I die, I will just shed my body. My spirit and my soul will continue to live eternally, and I will move into another level of existence. I won't have all the answers. I think that's why the universe was created, because_*God did create us, and He created us for Himself/Herself.* We are His/Her creation, and He might be our creation. We might have created each other. But God has always existed in spiritual form. If He did come down as Jesus, (there are no impossibilities when you're talking from the spiritual realm) then spirit was indeed made flesh.

Usually we are brought up in some faith. That's a good starting point. You start out there. Also, when you think about your existence - (your experience while you're here and your existence after you leave here) - there are certain moral obligations here society thinks that we should deal with if we're talking about it in a practical realm. In the

Christian and Judaic religions, it starts off with **The Ten Commandments** and you **look at those as sort of ways of living**.

The spiritual life is virtually a way of living where you are dealing with yourself and the people around you. I was brought up in the Christian faith, but there's a book by Houston Smith called <u>The Seven Basic Religions</u>, and I would implore people to get that book. It deals with every one of them - all the religions - the basic religions that there are, and it's not heavy reading, but it explains the philosophies of all of the religions. One of the spiritual needs of everybody is to live forever. **Everybody wants to live forever.** So at some point in time, you realize that you're going to have to leave this body here. Nobody has escaped with it yet - maybe Joshua or Ezekiel in the wheel - but those things will come into your being. Well, **how did I get here? Where did I come from, and where am I going?** Once you look at those things, these are spiritual questions because you're not going to take your body with you. Once you start trying to resolve those things, you will start asking questions. Now one of the best places to find the answers to those questions is to look at a book called The Religions of Man, which discusses all of the major and known religions. It even goes back to before there were structured religions, and it tells you what **things man has always wanted to have or do. He's always wanted wealth**, but even when he got wealth, he never had enough because the wealth wouldn't change him into another being, and he couldn't take it with him. So those questions will always be there.

I would think that a person who's trying to learn would go there first, if they really want to know, and just see the history of religions all the way up through the ones that they have and then look at the one that they're in, or if they are not in one.

There also is a discussion in this book on atheism – if you do not believe. But if you don't believe, what is it that you do believe? **You've got to believe something**. It might not be in religion; it might not be in God. It might be in science, but regardless of how you explain it, everything breaks down with the Big Bang. Steven Hawkings, who's one of the world's greatest physicists, has said there was a Big Bang. All the experts said that there was a Creation, and that may or may not be so, but it exists and in the physical world, things have a beginning and they have an ending. So where do you fit in the realm of things? A lot of people don't think about these things. **Think – think and re-think**.

Going too far with spirituality

We know that some people get out of balance with spirituality. They become obsessed. I would think probably a case like Jim Jones and the cults and maybe the Branch Davidians, although I'm not saying they did. It was all right for them. It would not have been all right for me. I'm not trying to put a limit on how far you can go or how far you can process. That's left up to you, but if you look at your life and how it affects you and how it affects the people around you, if you're **making other people better,** it's sort of like an athlete – **a good athlete** – a *good athlete makes his teammates better*. It's not about how good he is; he's able to bring the team along – to *make everybody else play better*. Wherever you go people will like to be around you because you make them feel and perform better.

Usually, when you go to extremes, at some point, you're out there but you've lost contact with the common people. *Jesus was always with the common people*. He always was able to relate to them. He always had ways in which he could teach them and make them better. *And that's what this book is for: TO MAKE YOU A BETTER PERSON*.

Individually, I think you have a right to go wherever you want to go, no matter what it might appear to be to other people. You might be a fanatic; you might be whatever you want to be. If you're happy in that, fine. But when you start to negatively affect other people, then I think you might need to check it. It's also up to other people to tell you that *"you're all right, but you take that over there or you keep it with yourself because I don't want any part of it. It disturbs me."* Or you can sit down and show them that "it might be right for you, but it's not right for me." That's okay if it's all right for you. You see, usually, if something is good for the international community, it's good for the immediate community. But just because something's good for the immediate community does not mean it's good for the broader population. So if there's a conflict, usually the international philosophy is going to really be the sort of benchmark. You've got to look at the way people have been socialized. Some people need the church and other organizations to help them because they don't have those skills to do that. I'm not saying that everybody should be individualistic or that people shouldn't be in cults. I'm not saying any of that. Whatever you feel comfortable with, that's where you should go. The structures that have passed on for years and years and organized religions are going to still exist. It's a great thing. I'm a member of the church, and I go, but still, individually, I have my own thoughts about spiritual things, and there are some things that I don't discuss personally with just anybody because the way that they're structured, it would create some needless problems for me and them.

In the end, life is all a paradox. How can something be created from nothing? It can, if you believe that it can. Faith is believing in something that isn't so until it is so. JUST BE WHATEVER YOU WANT TO BE.

- *THOUGHTS*
- *BELIEFS*
- *WORDS OF AFFIRMATION*
- *VISUALIZATION*
- *FAITH*
- *ACTION*
- *THE CREATION PROCESS*

Some things to do.

XII. SPIRITUALITY:

1. Write out your philosophy on spirituality.

2. Visit a faith-based place of worship other than your own.

3. Converse with people of faiths different from your own.

4. Give a copy of this book to your faith-based library to be kept on reserve.

5. Talk with the librarians. Get on-line. Do research.

6. Find a _good_ COACH.

7. Do what _you_ want to do!

MAKING IT ALL WORK TOGETHER

About now, you may be thinking, "Coach, there are an awful lot of new ideas in this book. How in the world can I remember all of them?" My wife and I developed the concepts and philosophies outlined in these chapters over a number of years, and we had to develop our own way of remembering them. After all, we're telling you that you need to consider the state of every critical element of your life on a regular daily basis.

We have always found that it helps to make up an acronym or some other easy way to remember things, so a few years ago, we developed one for this process: we tell ourselves every day to

Keep the emphasis on the "SPEMPP-FAR-SIS."

"Spemppfarsis" is one of my many made-up words, but it's very useful to me. Each letter stands for one of

the "Real Daily Dozen." It's a mnemonic acronym.

S- Social matters
P- Physical matters
E- Education
M- Mentality
P- Political matters
P- Professional matters
F- Financial matters
A- Attitude
R- Relationships
S- Sexuality
I- Imagination
S- Spirituality

EACH ONE, REACH ONE, TEACH ONE.
Now that we have this system, we find that it's much easier to check in on the various elements of our "SPEMPPFARSIS." My family understand the term, because we might tell them my "SPEMPPFARSIS" is off today. My students heard it enough times to understand it too. I'm offering it up as one easy way to remember what's really important. Whatever system you use, make it easy so you'll use it every day.

EMPHASIS ON THE "SPEMPPFARSIS"

CONCLUSION

In the beginning of this book, I told you what it wasn't: not a typical self-help book, or a health book, not a philosophy book, or a religion book. Yes, it covers all of those topics, but the point has been to make you think - not to give you answers. You may agree with many of the concepts here, or you may violently disagree. That's okay. The point is that you're thinking about them. ***God gave us choices, not answers.***

When you first started reading, you may have thought you didn't have any philosophies about the topics covered. Or you may have thought your philosophies were different than they are now that you've explored them. The point is you have a philosophy about things and you need to recognize it. It will guide you in so many ways.

Before you read this book, you may have been working hard at a job you didn't enjoy just in order to have enough money to buy things that you didn't even care about. Or you may have been busy raising children without really thinking about how you were shaping them for the rest of their lives. You may have been one of the millions of Americans who "sleepwalk" through their lives. Stop that.

The point of this book is that we all have to be accountable for our lives. Not only do we need to do the right things, but we also need to learn, grow, contribute to, and enjoy our lives continuously.

Every day, in every way, you are getting better and better and better. Keeping the emphasis on the "SPEMPPFARSIS" is one way of doing that.

Please **give** *as many books to as many people as you can financially afford to. Start with your family, friends, neighbors, co-workers, and members of other ethnic groups. Then give them to strangers that you think might profit from them.*

It is most beneficial to you that you give your spouse or significant other a copy of this book. Do not give him or her your copy.

After you both have finished reading it, sit down at times and

281

discuss each chapter. Write out your findings. Develop a written philosophy of your own for your family after each chapter. Discuss your philosophies with your other family members and members of other ethnic groups that have read the book.

Invite people of other ethnic groups to lunch to discuss different chapter philosophies. If you are comfortable with them, invite them and their families over for a cook out or family dinner. This should give you a starting point from which to improve race relations. It should go a long way in letting you know about racial fears and prejudices.

Books and Their Authors

1. *Men are from Mars, Women are from Venus*
    by Dr. John Gray

2. *The Religions of Man*
    by Huston Smith

3. *Passages*
    By Gail Sheehy